Three Screenplays
by
Edward Burns

Three Screenplays

by

Edward Burns

■

The Brothers McMullen

■

She's the One

■

No Looking Back

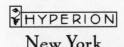

New York

LIBRARY OF CONGRESS CATALOGING-IN-PUBLICATION DATA
BURNS, EDWARD
  [SCREENPLAYS. SELECTIONS]
  THREE SCREENPLAYS / BY EDWARD BURNS. — 1ST ED.
    P.   CM.
  CONTENTS: THE BROTHERS MCMULLEN — SHE'S THE ONE — NO
LOOKING BACK.
  ISBN 0-7868-8272-7
  I. TITLE.
PS3552.U732438A6 1997
791.45′75—DC21   97–15616
                                                                    CIP

DESIGNED BY KATHY KIKKERT

FIRST EDITION

10 9 8 7 6 5 4 3 2 1

To my family
and everyone who was there
when I needed them.

Thank you.

Contents

◾

Introduction:

◾

It's about the process.

From the time I was twelve years old, all I ever wanted to do in life was play for the New York Knicks. I spent close to six hours a day, rain or shine, working on my jump shot. My friends and I would even shovel snow off the courts at Grant Park in order to get our daily fix. I figured I would follow in the footsteps of my hero, Chris Mullen, and be recruited by Lou Carnesecca and play for St. John's University. But, unlike Chris, I'd be drafted in the first round by my beloved Knickerbockers. Unfortunately, Mr. Carnesecca (who, incidentally, had cut my dad from the freshman team at St. Ann's Academy back in 1952) never made it out to Hewlett High School to see me play. For that matter, nobody from any Division I, II, or III schools came to see me play either. And so my basketball dream died a horrible death.

The following year, as a freshman at SUNY Albany, I declared myself an English major with the plan that I would go into sports journalism. If I couldn't play for the Knicks, at least I could write about them. While at school, I was hardly a model student. If I made it to campus once a week, it was a lot. So when I heard about a class called Film Appreciation that was a "guaranteed A," I quickly signed up. I should admit that at this time in my life I had little or no appreciation for film whatsoever. Prior to this course, my idea of a great film was any movie that included full frontal nudity. So, as you can imagine, my vote for Best Picture in 1982 was *Porky's*. But all that soon changed. During that one semester, we studied the films of Hitchcock, Welles, Ford, Wilder, and other masters, and my new dream was born.

I took every film class Albany had to offer, and my junior year I wrote my first screenplay, entitled "Apple Pie." Like most first screenplays, it was a semiautobiographical coming-of-age story, and I thought it was brilliant—so brilliant, in fact, that I could not send my masterpiece out to Hollywood and maybe have some hack misinterpret and massacre my vision. I needed somebody who truly understood this material. I decided I'd better learn how to make films. (Before I go on, I should say that I recently reread "Apple Pie" and have to admit it is less than brilliant.)

So I called my dad and told him about my new dream. I told him I'd be leaving Albany at the end of the year and enrolling in the NYU Film Program the following fall. He heard me out and then told me to look at my grades and look at his salary and suggested I rethink NYU. So I found Hunter College, part of the CUNY system in New York. With tuition at about six hundred dollars a semester, Hunter and I seemed like a perfect fit.

I know a lot of kids coming out of high school who want to study film think they have to attend one of the bigger film schools: NYU, UCLA, USC. But no school can teach you to be passionate or give you a personal vision or give you the guts to keep writing scripts when the rejection letters start piling up. (And let me speak from experience, they do pile up, a mile high.) What you need is a love of movies, a desire to learn everything you can about filmmaking, and, hopefully, a few professors who care about their students. That's what I had at Hunter College.

The first course I took was called Film Direction 101 with Professor Everett Aison. On the first day of class he asked us who was interested in becoming a director. The entire class raised their hands. He then asked if any of us had any acting experience. Four students raised their hands; I wasn't one of them. He then wondered, How did we expect to be able to tell actors what to do if we had never done any acting ourselves? He had a good point there. So at the start of every class he picked four students. One of us would be the writer, one the director, and the other two the actors. By the next class, the four of us were to present a scene to our fellow students. And by the end of the semester, everyone would have had an opportunity to get a taste of all three positions. That was my introduction to writing, directing, and acting.

While at Hunter, I made three short films, two of which were god-awful. The first one, though, entitled *Hey Sco,* isn't too shabby. It is a fifteen-minute black comedy about two Long Island losers who kill their best friend and bury him under the fifty-yard line at their old high school football field.

So I write the script for *Hey Sco* which I'm planning on directing. But before I could start shooting I obviously needed a cast. For some reason I was intimidated by the acting students in the theater department with their black turtlenecks and goatees. Rather than deal with them, I decided to cast myself (thinking I had done an alright job in Everett Aison's class last semester) and a friend from my editing class, Chris McGovern. (Just as a side note, Chris's part was cut out of *The Brothers McMullen* before shooting began, but he is slated to reprise his *Hey Sco* character, Sully, in *No Looking Back*.) After hitting my parents up for seven hundred dollars and getting a five-hundred-dollar grant from Hunter, a CP-16 (we heard this camera had been donated to the school after being used during WW II), a three-man crew, and one scheduled shooting day, I set out to make my first film. It was on a cold rainy October afternoon. We shot the fifteen-page script in six hours. And so my filmmaking career had begun.

I sent the film to every film festival in America, and it wasn't accepted anywhere. Still, I had the beginnings of what would soon become a fairly impressive collection of rejection letters.

I then submitted *Hey Sco* to the Independent Feature Film Market, which is held every September by the Independent Feature Project at the

Angelika Film Center in New York City. Unlike a festival, the market accepts almost every film submitted and ends up screening hundreds of movies, making it very difficult to get anyone other than other struggling filmmakers to see your film. However, nobody else had given me the opportunity to see my film thrown up against a screen in a theater. So when they accepted me, I was overjoyed.

The day of the screening I posted flyers for the film all over the Angelika Film Center and on every mailbox, phone booth, and telephone pole on Houston Street. (Every few hours I would have to go back and repost my flyers because other filmmakers with a screening that day had posted their flyers over mine.)

When my time finally arrived, I stood in the back of the theater as the lights dimmed and the opening credits appeared on the screen. Seeing your first film play on the screen in front of you is one of the most exciting, and at the same time terrifying, experiences imaginable. Unfortunately, I didn't set the world on fire that day, but watching images I created and listening to the words I wrote was one of the highlights of my life. My dream was now a reality. I was a filmmaker.

After taking every film course Hunter had to offer, I left school to find a job in the "entertainment business." For four years I worked as a production assistant at the New York bureau of *Entertainment Tonight*. My main responsibilities there included driving the crew around Manhattan from location to location, carrying the lights and tripod, and getting coffee for whoever asked. The one advantage to the gig was that in between shoots I was free to do as I pleased. I took advantage of this downtime by holing up in an empty office and writing screenplays. I wrote four screenplays my first two years there and sent them out to any agent, producer, production company, or manager whose address I could track down.

You should know that the really tough part about screenplay writing is not the writing but finding anyone in the business who will read your script—unless it is submitted to them by an agent. "Hey, jerkoff," I admit I occasionally said. "If I already had an agent, why would I bother sending you my script in the first place?" (I have to confess, that reaction rarely got me anywhere, but at least it felt good.) Apparently, however, there is some legal reason why industry pros can't accept unsolicited scripts. So the

Catch-22 is you can't sell a script unless you have an agent, and you can't get an agent unless you've sold a script. Welcome to Hollywood.

Nevertheless, I was determined to get my foot in the door. I thought if I took one step every day to get me closer, I would eventually find my way through that door. So every day I either wrote a new scene, hunted down another potential agent, wrote another pleading letter, or made one more desperate phone call. I got about three nibbles and two hundred more rejection letters to add to the collection. By then I'm feeling like a loser.

It's been almost three years since I've made *Hey Sco,* I'm not getting anywhere as a writer, and John Tesh still doesn't know my name. (John Tesh, the former host of *Entertainment Tonight,* was based in LA, so there was no real reason for him to know who I was anyway.)

My dad decides to take me out for a meal to cheer me up, or so I think. We meet down at the White Horse in the West Village for a burger and a few beers. I start to piss and moan and feel sorry for myself. I go on about how Hollywood sucks and bitch about how they're not giving me a shot. So he says to me, If you're a filmmaker, why don't you just make a film? Why do you need Hollywood? I try to tell him that it's not that easy; I'd need at least a million dollars. He says that's bullshit. How much did *Hey Sco* cost? I say close to three thousand in the end. Then he asks how long the film was, and I tell him fifteen minutes. So he asks, Why can't you make a ninety-minute film that costs eighteen thousand if *Hey Sco* cost three thousand? I said I hadn't thought about it that way. He then told me to get off my ass, stop my crying, and write a script we could make for eighteen thousand. The next day at work—between shoots, of course—I sat down and started writing *The Brothers McMullen.*

At about this time, Nick Gomez's *Laws of Gravity* and Whit Stillman's *Metropolitan* had just been released. Those films' budgets were about $40,000 and $200,000 respectively. I used them as motivation and inspiration. The first thing I did was think of locations I knew I could get for free. They included my parents' house, my friends' apartments, Central Park, and New York City streets. I knew from experience that casting can be difficult in no-budget filmmaking. When hiring actors who will work for free, the young independent filmmaker must realize that if a paying gig comes along for your lead actor, whether it's an acting job or a waitering job, chances are your film will take a backseat. That's when I decided not only to cast myself in one of the leads—at least I would show up every day—but also to write an ensemble piece. In a crunch, I could always write the unavailable actor's character out of the film and the available actor's character in (and during shooting this happened more than once). So with that in mind, I started to think about my story.

Growing up Irish Catholic, my friends and I always wondered why movies were never made that took a look at our lives and the people we grew up with. Any Irish American can tell you what a colorful bunch we are. We saw that Italian Americans had Scorsese and Coppola, Jewish Americans had Woody Allen and Barry Levinson, and African Americans had Spike Lee and later John Singleton and the Hughes Brothers. So I knew I wanted to take a look at what it was like to grow up Irish Catholic in New York. The other topic I was hungry to explore was the relationship between brothers and to have some fun with the conversations brothers have with one another that they would never have with their friends, parents, sisters, girlfriends, or wives. Maybe I could even make it funny.

I finished the first draft three months later and put together a bare-bones budget of $25,000 that covered the cost of the film stock and the film processing. Everything else, including the actors, the crew, the camera, the sound equipment, and the locations, would have to be deferred or gotten for free. With the help of our lawyer, Paul Derounian, my dad and I put together a limited partnership agreement selling $5,000 partnerships. My dad and one of his buddies, Bill Tierney, were the only two investors we could find. That was the end of our limited partnership. But I convinced Bill and my dad to give me their $10,000 and let me get started. I would shoot a few scenes and cut together a trailer and use that to raise the rest of the money. They agreed.

Dick Fisher, a cameraman I was working with at *Entertainment Tonight,* agreed to shoot the film and lend the production his camera, sound equipment, car, apartment, and almost everything else he owned. The rest of the crew was filled out by friends who were good enough to give me their time for free. I don't think anybody who worked on the film expected to see their deferred pay. It felt more like a group of people who were having a good time trying to create something special. I was lucky enough to have friends like that. If the film never sold, I knew I'd be paying back favors for the rest of my life.

Next up was casting. I placed an ad in *Back Stage* magazine: "No-Budget Feature Seeks Irish Brothers—No Pay—Meals Included." I received close to fifteen hundred head shots in three weeks. I thought, Wow, this is going to be easy! That proved not to be the case.

We started shooting in October 1993, and it was tough going. You can imagine how hard it is to coordinate getting a free location, a crew, equipment, and a cast together for one day when you can only pay people with the promise of two slices of pizza for lunch. Over the course of the next three months, we only had six shooting days. However, by that point we had gotten more than half the film in the can. Shooting close to twelve pages a day with almost no coverage, the actors were given three to four takes, tops, to get a scene. If we didn't get it, we had no choice but to move on. We also couldn't afford dailies after each shooting day, so after three months we really had no idea what we had. That, combined with the fact that we were shooting on recanned 16mm film stock (recanned film stock is film that has been left over from someone else's shoot, usually a music video, placed back in the can, and sold at a discount to poor bastards like us) can be pretty scary. But I have to admit, those six days were the greatest six days of my life.

Then disaster struck. The $10,000 ran out just as I went into the hospital for an emergency appendectomy. The day I got out of the hospital, Dick Fisher slipped a disk in his back, keeping him laid up for almost a month. All of this was bookended by two of the worst snowstorms New York had seen in years. Originally, I had told the cast we would be done shooting by early November; then I pushed it to late December. Now it's March and they're growing restless. We hadn't shot anything in close to three months, and we had no more money. But we had become a tight-knit group and something of a family. So we all got together at Jack Mulcahy's apartment to regroup. (For whatever it's worth, I should note that one of Jack's first film roles was in *Porky's,* a good omen.) They assured me they're in this for the long haul and will see the film through to the end. Or at least for a few more months. So I hit up the old man for another five thousand, and then Irwin Young at DuArt Film Labs really saved the day by allowing us to defer the rest of our processing costs. Our first day back shooting was Saint Patrick's Day, another good omen.

We shot another twelve days over the next six weeks and wrapped the film in late April, eight months after we started.

Dick and I then edited the film during the following months and transferred a two-hour cut to VHS. I sent copies to every distribution company, big and small, including Miramax, New Line, October, Paramount, Sony Classics, and Sam Goldwyn. All I got back were more rejection letters to add to my collection. And they all said basically the same thing: "Although your film shows promise, it does not fit into our distribution needs at this time." So I sent it out to all the agents who had rejected my earlier screenplays and the response was, "Although your film shows promise, I am unable to sign any new clients at this time." So I tried the festival route: Telluride, New Directors, New York; even the Hamptons Film Festival turned me down. And I'm from Long Island, for Christ's sake! The letters generally said something like, "Although your film shows great promise for an 'Independent' film, we found it wasn't 'edgy' enough for our festival." My rejection letter collection, needless to say, grew even bigger.

So I meet my dad down at the White Horse Tavern again for a few beers and to talk about my future as a filmmaker. Again, my dad listens quietly as I piss and moan about how unfairly the festivals and the distribution companies and the agents have treated me and how I am at the end of my rope and what am I going to do? He asks me if I'd like to take the cops test at the end of the month. I, of course, say no. So he tells me to stop my pissing and moaning. He asks me if I enjoyed the process of making *The Brothers McMullen*. I tell him it was the greatest experience of my life. So he asks why am I bitching. I tell him because I want to be a filmmaker. He asks me if I made a film. I say, Yeah. He says, So you're a filmmaker. I try to tell him it's not the same thing. He says, Shut up. He says, If you're doing this writing and directing because this is how you have to express yourself and because you enjoy it, why the fuck would you give a shit what those assholes out in Hollywood think about your work? If you really enjoyed the process as much as you say you did, go out and make another film. And if they don't like that one, go out and make another one after that. And keep making films until you have nothing left to say. But if you're doing this because you want to be a big Hollywood hotshot and make a lot of money and go to parties with those assholes, then I don't want to know you. And I'll never invest in another one of your movies. But if you're doing this because you love it, write another script and we'll find a way to get you the money. That night, I started writing *She's the One*.

A few weeks later, my luck changed. I had submitted *McMullen* to the Independent Feature Film Market as a work in progress. Bob Hawk, my first fan and early supporter, saw the film and told journalist Amy Taubin from the *Village Voice* to check it out. In her post-Market article she gave the film a nice mention (the first and last time I expect the *Voice* to do so), and her only criticism was regarding the film's "blatant commercial appeal." I thought I could deal with criticism like that, so I sent *McMullen* back out to the same distribution companies with Amy's article attached. More rejection letters followed, but I could feel the ball starting to roll.

Through a friend, we had also gotten a copy of the film to David Evans, an executive in Twentieth Century–Fox's Television Department. David loved the film and took a personal interest in it. He sent it along to Tom Rothman, who was starting up Fox Searchlight, a new specialty film division at the studio. Tom liked it and gave me a call. He told me that although he loved the film, Searchlight wasn't on its feet and couldn't help me out just yet, but we should keep in touch.

I then got the film to Ted Hope and James Shamus from Good Machine, a New York–based independent production company. They liked the film and wanted to help. They came on board as executive producers and sales agents and helped me cut the film down to its current 98-minute running time. Right around then I realized that I would be needing an entertainment attorney to handle the legal side of things, and I met a great guy named John Sloss, who represented John Sayles, one of my heroes. So we hired him.

And the ball kept rolling. On November 12, 1994, I got a call from Geoff Gilmore of the Sundance Film Festival. Geoff gave me the best news of my life, *The Brothers McMullen* had been accepted into the main competition. But now we had a problem: the festival was two months away, we were out of money, and we needed to finish cutting the film and blow it up from 16mm to 35mm. So we called our friend, Tom Rothman, over at Fox Searchlight. Tom agreed to offer us a first-look deal on the film. With that money we finished our film two days before it was to premiere in Park City, Utah.

Before the first Sundance screening began, Bob Hawk stood on the stage and introduced me and the film. I sat in the back row at the Egyptian Theater on Main Street as the lights dimmed and the credits started to roll. Because we had only really finished the film a few days earlier, this was the first time I would see it projected on a screen from start to finish. I have since sat and watched both *The Brothers McMullen* and *She's the One* in sold-out movie theaters in San Francisco; Washington, D.C.; London; San Sebastián, Spain; Deauville, France; and Hamburg, Germany; but nothing will ever compare to the thrill of sitting in the back row on that cold January afternoon.

Nobody in that theater had ever heard of me or heard of the film. They went in with no expectations. But during the first scene when Mrs. McMullen tells her son she's going back to Ireland for her long-lost love, the audience started to laugh, and they continued to laugh. About halfway through the film, I must have looked like a wreck because an old woman sitting next to me grabbed my knee and said, "Don't worry, they love it." When the film ended, there was excitement in the room that I can't imagine I'll ever experience again. I knew my life would never be the same.

Immediately following the screening I was rushed by a horde of Hollywood types. I received close to two hundred business cards from agents, producers, and managers, all promising me the world. Of course, we would have to do lunch first. And when would I be in LA. Or, for that matter, you know, you really should move to LA. I later took those business cards and matched them up to my rejection-letter collection. It was an easy way of weeding through who I wouldn't be signing with.

That night, we sold the film to Tom Rothman and Fox Searchlight, and a month later they gave a green light to *She's the One*.

Now, as I write this introduction, it is late February 1997—almost two years to the date of that memorable Sundance Film Festival—and we're gearing up to begin the process all over again with *No Looking Back*.

—Edward Burns
New York City

Editor's Note

▫

The screenplays for *The Brothers McMullen* and *She's the One* are transcribed from the films as they were theatrically released. The script for *No Looking Back* is the shooting draft used prior to filming and, as such, may differ from the final theatrical version.

The Brothers McMullen

Fade in:

◼ EXT: CALVARY GRAVEYARD (QUEENS, N.Y.). DAY

A gray day. The crowd from the funeral has cleared out. MRS. McMULLEN, dressed in black, pulls her son BARRY aside.

MRS. McMULLEN
Finbar, come here. . . .

BARRY
Come on, Ma, don't call me Finbar, all right?

MRS. McMULLEN
Finbar, I'm telling you because you're the only one who'll understand, so you'll have to tell your brothers.

BARRY
Understand what? What's going on?

MRS. McMULLEN
I'm leaving.

BARRY
What do you mean, you're leaving?

MRS. McMULLEN

Your father's dead and buried now and . . . I gave him the best years of my life, but now I have to go and live the rest of my life.

BARRY

What . . . what the hell are you talking about?

MRS. McMULLEN

Watch your mouth! I'm going back to Ireland.

BARRY

For . . . for Mr. O'Shaughnessy?

MRS. McMULLEN

I love him, Finbar. I've loved him my whole life.

BARRY

Do . . . does . . . like, you know, does he even know you're coming?

MRS. McMULLEN

Of course he knows. He's been waiting thirty-five years for this day. Now come give your mom a kiss. I have a plane to catch.

MRS. McMULLEN holds her son's face in her hands and gives him a kiss.

BARRY

Are you sure you're going to be all right?

MRS. McMULLEN

I'm going to be fine, darling. And tell your brothers I'll explain everything when I call next week.
(beat)
And promise me you won't make the same mistake I made.

BARRY

Yeah. I promise.

MRS. McMULLEN

Good boy.

MRS. McMULLEN then turns and walks away from BARRY down a path toward her car.

                          BARRY
          Good luck, Mom.

MRS. McMULLEN turns and waves. BARRY watches as she disappears down the path.

Fade to black.

Titles appear.

Five years later.

◻EXT: McMULLEN HOUSE. DAY

A sunny fall day. The three McMullen brothers, BARRY, JACK, and PATRICK, sit on their front stoop drinking beers. Their home is a typical one-family house in a working-class Long Island neighborhood. An American flag flaps in the breeze.

IAN TONG

JACK

Cheers.

BARRY AND PATRICK

Cheers.

The three guys toast with their beers.

JACK

So Barry, let me ask you . . . what's up with you and Heather?
You've got this new one here in the house now. . . . What, you
guys are all done?

BARRY

I don't . . . you know . . . I mean, just like any long
relationship—

PATRICK
(cutting him off)
Long relationship? You were with her for six months.

BARRY

Yeah, well, that's a long time, you know. . . . I mean . . . you
know, the mystery was over, man. I don't know why that
happens.

PATRICK

It's God's way of testing you, Barry. You're failing.

BARRY

Yeah, he loves to torture us.

PATRICK

Oh, so you believe in God now? This is . . . this is your
story?

BARRY

Well, yeah . . . yeah, on his good days.

PATRICK

Then you're not a Catholic anymore.

BARRY

No, I'm ... I'm still a Catholic ... I guess. ... You know ...
kind of.

JACK

Catholic? Who the hell are you kidding? You haven't been in
church since tenth grade!

BARRY

Yeah, but you know, who can deal with all that repression
anyhow?

PATRICK

Hey, hey, repression is not such a bad thing, okay? Especially for
a savage like you. So, when did all this happen? I mean, what did
she do, as I'm positive it's her fault completely.

BARRY

You know, she started talking about getting married.

JACK

Marriage? Jesus, and what did you say?

BARRY

I asked her, you know, who she was planning on marrying and
if ... you know, she'd be kind enough to invite me to the
wedding.

PATRICK

You said that to her? Good for her, I'm glad she threw you out.
So? Where are you going to live now, Mister Hotshot
Noncommittal?

BARRY

I ... I don't know, man.

BARRY gives JACK a look asking for help.

JACK

Don't even think about it!

BARRY

Yeah, like I might ever live with this joker, right? No, I'm going
to look for a place down in the Village tomorrow, I think.

JACK

Oh, the Village, huh? That's about your speed.

BARRY

Yeah, right.

PATRICK
(standing up)
We better get in; Molly's probably got dinner ready for us.

PATRICK *heads into the house, followed by* BARRY. *They both leave their
empty beer bottles on the steps for* JACK *to grab before he enters.*

◘ INT: DINING ROOM. DAY (CONT)

BARRY *enters from the kitchen and sits down at the table.* JACK *sits at the
head of the table across from his wife,* MOLLY. PATRICK *sits opposite*
BARRY *and* ANN, *Barry's date, with his own girlfriend,* SUSAN.

SUSAN

Look, you know, I don't care what anybody says, it doesn't make
a difference to me if he did or he didn't, right? All I can say is,
thank you for giving us John Jr.! I saw him jogging through the
park yesterday—now there is a real man!

BARRY

Sounds like she really loves you, pal.

PATRICK

Oh, yeah, totally. . . . I think Molly's right.

MOLLY

Thank you, Patrick.

JACK

Wait, wha . . . what are you saying? You don't like JFK now? The
only Irish Catholic president of this great country of ours, and
now you don't like him?

MOLLY

Listen. I don't . . . I don't care. I don't care who the guy is, I don't care what kind of great stuff he's done. I don't like a man who cheats on his wife. Period.

JACK

Oh, that's all just bullshit rumors. I mean, the man was a great man.

ANN

Well, even if he did, that doesn't necessarily make him bad.

BARRY

The man was the President of the United States; I mean, he's under a lot of pressure. I think he was entitled! Besides, he screwed around with Marilyn Monroe. I think it's the sign of a . . . truly great individual who knows how to seize an opportunity like that.

MOLLY

You're demented, Barry.

PATRICK

Ahh. . . . This is thinking, this is a thought process.

SUSAN

Thank you for dinner, Molly, it was delicious.

BARRY

Yeah, that corned beef and cabbage was . . . very close second to our mother's.

MOLLY

Well, I hate to tell you guys this but . . . Jack made the dinner.

PATRICK

Jackie, an all-star in the kitchen too; Barry, get this.

JACK

See? This just goes to show how little my brothers actually know about me. I mean, they probably see me like my dad, which was—

BARRY
(cutting him off)
Speaking of our favorite wife-beating, child-abusing alcoholic,
I . . . I went down to the grave this morning . . .

JACK
And?

BARRY
And . . . I'm happy to report that . . . he's still dead.

PATRICK
This is . . . this is funny stuff, Barry. Take it on the road, pal.

JACK looks at BARRY and shakes his head disapprovingly, thinking "asshole."

JACK
Anyway, see, these guys, they see me as this old-fashioned,
conservative, by-the-book kind of guy when in actuality I'm a
progressively modern, politically correct housewife.

BARRY
(doing his best Archie Bunker)
You sound more like half a fag there, Edith.

PATRICK
Hey, I can see you, you know, wearing an apron, you know,
with the skirt and those heavy clogs you like to wear, maybe a
Speedo thrown in there for the added effect. What do you
think?

JACK
I think I'm gonna throw the two of you a beating, that's what I
think.

MOLLY
Listen, you guys, it's true, he does: he cooks, he cleans, he does
the laundry. Leaves me all kinds of time for all those things I
always wanted to do . . . like change the oil in the car and fix the
sink and mow the lawn.

JACK
(stands up)
I'd like to propose a toast: to Molly, my lawn-mowing, oil-changing, sink-fixing, beautiful, sweet, smart, sexy, sassy, one-in-a-million Irish lass on her thirtieth birthday. . . . That means stand up, people. . . . Come on, get up.

The others at the table stand, raising their glasses.

JACK
I love you, and although I missed the first twenty-five of your thirty years, here's hoping that you'll keep me around for another thirty. Happy Birthday!

ALL
Happy Birthday, Molly!

The group toasts. ANN gives JACK a sexy glance. He quickly looks away.

◾INT: KITCHEN. SAME DAY

PATRICK stands at the dishwasher with a dirty dish in his hands, trying to crane his neck out the kitchen window to watch LESLIE, a neighborhood girl, walking down the street across from the house. BARRY walks in on PATRICK.

BARRY
What are you doing?

PATRICK quickly turns around with the dish still in his hands.

PATRICK
Nothing. Let me ask you something, Barry. . . . What do I do now, huh?

BARRY
(referring to the dish)
What are you, retarded? You wipe it off, and then you put it in the dishwasher. Okay, genius?

PATRICK

No, not with . . . I mean with my life. . . . You know, I didn't
think college would actually end. I'm not ready to go out and be
a real guy, get a . . . get a real job. I'm not ready to move out of
my dorm. Do you know, I didn't even think about that. Where
the hell am I going to live?

BARRY

What the hell are you worried about? I mean, Susan told me
that her father has already got a job lined up for you.

PATRICK

I know, I . . . I don't know if I should take it. Susan's starting to
scare me a little bit too.

BARRY

Yeah, well, Susan does have that effect on people.

BARRY crosses over to the fridge and opens it.

PATRICK

The other night, Barry, you know, we're in my room, we're in
my dorm room, doing it. . . .

Cut to flashback:

◘INT: DORM ROOM. NIGHT

PATRICK and SUSAN in bed having sex. PATRICK is on top.

PATRICK

Don't move. . . .

SUSAN

What?

PATRICK
(reaching under the covers)
Don't move. I think I broke it.

SUSAN

Oh, God.

PATRICK

Oh . . . Pfff. . . .

SUSAN

Don't. . . .

PATRICK

Oh, thank God, that was close. They make these things so
tight. . . . Why don't they make them bigger for guys like
me?

SUSAN

Shut up.

PATRICK

Yeah, you know that, baby. . . .

SUSAN

Yeah, right. . . . I . . . you know, I don't even know why you
bother with those. I'm on the pill!

PATRICK

Hey, hey, you can't be too careful. And remember I'm Catholic;
I shouldn't be doing this in the first place.

SUSAN

You know, we wouldn't even have to worry about it if we got
married.

Cut back to:

◼ INT: KITCHEN. SAME DAY (CONT)

BARRY and PATRICK are where we left them.

BARRY

She said that? Married? Is she crazy?

PATRICK

Yeah. Yeah, I think so. So what do I do about this now?

BARRY

You got to break up with her. I mean, you got to dump her. Before you know it she's gonna have you picking out wedding cakes; you'll be asking me to be your best man, and moving into the guest bedroom of her parents' apartment, or, worse than that, moving up into our old room in the attic.

PATRICK

So you think I should break up with her?

BARRY

Yeah, you got to.

◘EXT: WEST 72ND STREET. EVENING

JACK'S Ford LTD pulls up outside ANN'S prewar apartment building.

◘INT: JACK'S CAR. EVENING (CONT)

JACK and ANN sit in the front seat. Neither one seems to be in any hurry to leave.

ANN

Thanks for driving me all the way into the city, Jack. I mean, you really didn't have to do that.

JACK

Hey, no problem. I mean, Barry and half a bottle of Irish whiskey is not my idea of safe driving.

ANN

So, other than cook corned beef and cabbage on his wife's birthday, what does a high school basketball coach do with his spare time?

JACK

Oh . . . things like . . . play golf, fish, drink a lot of beers. But I'm actually taking a sports management course in NYU at the moment.

ANN
(sarcastically)
Oh, very exciting. . . . And . . . Molly, what does she do?

JACK
She teaches English at the high school.

ANN
She's a teacher too. . . . Really exciting. What, did you two meet
at a PTA meeting or something?

JACK
No, it was . . . it was actually during cafeteria duty.

ANN
In the hot-lunch line, I hope.

JACK
Yeah, something like that.

ANN
Uh, I'll . . . bet you were a big jock stud in high school, weren't
you? Running around in the backseat of your father's Buick,
breaking all the little girls' hearts?

JACK
No, I've . . . I've always been pretty much a one-woman kind of
guy.

ANN
That's what my ex-husband said when I met him.

JACK
And he wasn't?

ANN
No, he was. . . . I just wasn't a one-man kind of girl.

JACK
I don't buy that. Your problem is that you just haven't found the
right man yet.

ANN

I've found plenty of them. My problem is that they all want to marry me. You know, if I was smart, I'd find myself a nice married man.

JACK

What good would that do you?

ANN

Because then there would be no question as to what either one of us wanted from the relationship . . . now, would there?

JACK knows where this is headed and doesn't appear all that comfortable. He takes a look at his watch.

ANN

Yeah, it's getting late.

JACK

Yeah.

ANN

Do you feel like coming up for a cup of coffee or something?

JACK

Oh. . . . No, thanks. I should be getting back to the Island . . . traffic and stuff. . . .

ANN

All right, some other time then.

JACK

Yeah, some other time.

ANN

Okay, some other time.

JACK

Okay.

ANN

Thanks for the ride, Jack.

Ann leans over and gives Jack a quick kiss.

ANN

Have a good night.

JACK

'Bye.

◻EXT: WEST VILLAGE STREETS. DAY

A montage of Barry's apartment hunt:

—BARRY, with the apartment listings in hand, in a corner phone booth getting no answer.

—BARRY exiting an apartment building, disappointed.

—BARRY finding no one answering the door at another building and walking off the front stoop, defeated.

BARRY approaches one last building. As he climbs the stoop, he meets AUDREY, heading down the stoop. She wears glasses and a baseball cap.

BARRY

Excuse me.

AUDREY

Yeah?

BARRY

You're not Mrs. McKay, are you?

AUDREY

No, she just left.

BARRY

What do you mean she just left?

AUDREY

I mean she was here a minute ago and now she's not.

BARRY

Well, do you know where she went? I mean, she was supposed
to show me an apartment in this building.

AUDREY

Oh, you're the one.

BARRY

What is that supposed to mean? I'm the one what?

AUDREY

She wanted to get out of here before you got here.

BARRY

Why? What the hell did I do?

AUDREY

She said you sounded a little crazy on the telephone. She didn't
want to face you.

BARRY

Me, crazy? She's the crazy one. Who does business like this? . . .
Well, do you know where she went? I mean, maybe she'll show
it to me after she meets me.

AUDREY

No, she already rented it; that's why she felt bad.

BARRY

I just spoke to her ten minutes ago. Who could she have rented
it to in that time?

AUDREY

Me.

*AUDREY spins on her heels and makes her way down the tree-lined street.
BARRY quickly follows.*

BARRY

You! So you stole my apartment?

AUDREY

That's not a very nice way to put it.

BARRY

Well, I'm not feeling very nice at this particular moment, you know? I've been looking at apartments all day, none of which I could afford, and this one was finally in my ballpark.

AUDREY

C'est la vie!

BARRY

You know, you should really let me look at it and then we could bid on it. That would be fair.

AUDREY

Who ever told you that life is fair? Good-bye!

BARRY

You know . . . hold up a second. I'm really sorry. . . . My name is Barry.

AUDREY stops. She doesn't want to deal with him but he won't give up.

AUDREY

Hello, Barry.

BARRY

Um, I was thinking, why don't we go out for a cup of coffee or something and maybe work something out?

AUDREY

Thank you, Barry. But I'm a married woman.

BARRY

You're married?

AUDREY

Yes, and I don't think my husband would appreciate me going out for drinks with a strange man. Now good-bye.

AUDREY turns and leaves BARRY standing alone on the sidewalk.

BARRY
(VO)

Oh, man, I'm a complete loser.

◨EXT: WEST 81ST STREET. DAY

SUSAN and PATRICK pull up in front of a typical Upper West Side brownstone; SUSAN is driving. They get out of the car and head toward the front stoop.

SUSAN

You are going to love this place, Patrick. It's only a one-bedroom, but Daddy says it's big enough for the both of us. Get this, honey, he paid for the first six months of rent. He got it through this friend of his. . . . It's going to be great until we get married; then we can move to a two-bedroom on the fourth floor.

PATRICK

I can't do it.

SUSAN

Can't do what?

PATRICK

I can't move into this apartment with you.

SUSAN

Why not? It's perfect.

PATRICK

I'm sure it is, but ethically, morally, I can't do it. I can't live with a woman I'm not married to. I mean, I would need for us to get married in order for me to feel comfortable with this.

SUSAN

But we're going to get married eventually, right? So what's the difference?

PATRICK

The difference is we are not married now and therefore I would be living in sin.

SUSAN

But we're not living in sin, we love each other!

PATRICK

What is that? What does that mean? Listen, there is no amendment to the rule, living in sin lest you love . . . okay? I can't do it, all right? That's the bottom line.

SUSAN

I know what you're doing here, you know. I know that you're just . . . you're afraid of making a commitment like that, you don't want to live with me, so you're using this as an excuse 'cause you . . . you're not willing to make a commitment like that, are you?

PATRICK

No, no, Susan, it's not that, I swear!

SUSAN

Then what is it?

PATRICK

It's . . . I'm a Catholic, that's what it is. And there's certain rules and regulations you got to live by. I'm living by 'em. Hey, for the same reason you won't eat a bacon cheeseburger, this is a part of my baggage.

SUSAN

Well, then, I really think that you should consider converting because Daddy is going to be very upset.

SUSAN storms away from PATRICK.

▣ INT: SUBWAY STATION. SAME DAY

PATRICK steps onto the train and sits down.

▣ INT: TRAIN. SAME DAY (CONT)

PATRICK sits alone and confused on the train.

PATRICK
(VO)

She's right, isn't she? Am I using this living-in-sin thing because I really don't want to live with her? But do I really believe I should wait until I'm married? Yeah, but if . . . if I obeyed every rule that says I should wait till I get married—well, I'd still be a virgin . . . and is that any way to go through life?

◘INT: JACK AND MOLLY'S LIVING ROOM. DAY

BARRY and PATRICK sit on the living room couch, their suitcases before them. JACK, arms folded, stands above them. He is not too happy with this visit.

BARRY

I can't speak for Sally boy over here, but for me, a few weeks . . . a month. A month, tops.

PATRICK

I don't know . . . definitely longer than a few weeks. A month or . . . Thanksgiving.

BARRY

Yeah, Thanksgiving is definitely the latest I'm here.

JACK

Thanksgiving?

BARRY

Well, maybe . . . maybe not Thanksgiving. . . . How about . . . how about Christmas? Yeah, Christmas will be the latest I'm here.

PATRICK

New Year's. Definitely no longer than New Year's.

BARRY

Hey, Jack, I promise you I will not be here a day after the new year, not a minute.

PATRICK

Not a second after the clock strikes twelve.

JACK
(giving in)
Okay, you can stay. Take your old room up in the attic. It still has all your old furniture and shit in it, okay?

BARRY *slaps* PATRICK *on the knee. They're in.*

◻INT: JACK AND MOLLY'S BEDROOM. NIGHT

JACK *walks into the bedroom and sits on the bed.* MOLLY *lies behind him, reading.*

JACK
I know I'm going to end up killing one of those guys.

MOLLY
Oh, you know what? I almost forgot to tell you. Ann called . . .

JACK
. . . ah–ha . . .

MOLLY
. . . to thank you for the dinner and for driving her home. She seemed like such a nice lady, don't you think?

JACK
I suppose.

MOLLY
Shame Barry doesn't like her. . . .

JACK
Hey, Barry doesn't like himself. Are you sure you're going to be okay with all this?

MOLLY
Jack, they're your brothers. You don't say no to family. I would do anything for them. Of course, if . . . Patrick decides to start wearing my underwear . . .

JACK

. . . which he might . . .

MOLLY

. . . which he might. . . . Besides, I think . . . I think we ought to start getting used to having to share this house with some other people.

JACK

I've already had plenty of practice in that department, thank you very much.

JACK gets up off the bed and walks to his closet. MOLLY follows.

MOLLY

Well, you know, I'm not getting any younger, Jack. And you said that we'd be having kids before I turned thirty. And in case you forgot, I turned thirty last week, and the only kids running around here are already in their twenties.

JACK

Come on, Molly. Kids are a big step.

MOLLY
(grabbing his hands)
I know that . . . but I'm ready to make that step. I don't care if we have to make a few sacrifices.

JACK

Look, kids need money for food and clothing, medication. Do you know what that means? It means no more vacations to Ireland to see your grandmother or my mother, no more trips to Aruba during winter recess. No more restaurants. We won't be able to afford it.

MOLLY

Well, good, because I can't stand my grandmother, I hate Aruba, and I'd rather cook. I want a family, Jack. I want a house that's teeming with little kids running up and down the stairs. You know, I want to cheer for them at baseball games and hold them when they scrape their knees. . . . You said that's what you wanted too.

JACK

I do, I do. . . . I'm not . . . I still want those things. I just don't want to rush into it, you know. I just . . . just need to know that we're ready.

MOLLY

I'm ready, Jack. You let me know when you are too.

MOLLY heads out of the bedroom.

◼EXT: WEST VILLAGE STREET CORNER. DAY

BARRY approaches the corner and is stopped by AUDREY. However, without her glasses and baseball hat, she is barely recognizable from the first time we've seen her.

AUDREY

Excuse me, do you know where 121 Jane Street is?

BARRY

Yeah, 121 . . . I think is down this way. Hey, do I know you from somewhere?

AUDREY
(ignoring his question)

Are you sure? I've got a commercial audition there that I'm already late for.

BARRY

Yeah, I'm pretty sure. . . . I know that I know you from somewhere. Did we—uh . . .

AUDREY

Do you mind walking me? I've been up and down this block five times. I just can't seem to make any sense of the streets down here.

BARRY

Yeah, sure.

◼EXT: JANE STREET. DAY (CONT)

BARRY and AUDREY head down the street, searching for the address.

> BARRY
>
> Well, that's 121 right over there.

> AUDREY
>
> Oh, great. Hey, thanks again. I hope I didn't put you out of your way.

> BARRY
>
> No, not at all.

> AUDREY
> *(suddenly recognizing him)*
>
> Hey, I know where I know you from. You're the creep who wanted to rent my apartment.

> BARRY
>
> Oh, my God, that's you? You look so different now.

> AUDREY
>
> You kept bugging me to go out with you.

> BARRY
>
> I didn't keep bugging you. . . . I think I just asked you once to go out for a cup of coffee.

> AUDREY
>
> And I told you that I was married.

> BARRY
>
> You're not?

> AUDREY
>
> No, I just said that to get rid of you.

> BARRY
>
> Why would you want to get rid of me?

AUDREY

Because first of all you accused me of stealing your apartment, and second of all I was told never to go out with strange men.

BARRY

Well, you know, I mean . . . I'm not exactly a stranger anymore, you know; I did help you find this place.

AUDREY

And third, I'm engaged.

BARRY

Engaged?

AUDREY

To be married . . . to Henry, who happens to be a very nice young man. Now, how do I look?

BARRY

Absolutely beautiful.

AUDREY

Thanks.

AUDREY smiles and waves and skips across the street to her audition.

◘INT: MCMULLEN BASEMENT. NIGHT

BARRY sucks on a beer in the laundry room and watches JACK fold their laundry.

BARRY

I'm telling you, Jack, she was beautiful.

JACK

And she didn't fall for your phony Irish charm, eh?

BARRY

She didn't give me the time of day. You know I was thinking, you know, she'd feel bad for me, maybe invite me to move in with her.

JACK

Why should she feel bad for you?

BARRY

Because she stole the apartment right out from under me. So instead of living down in the Village, I'm out here on Long Island with, you know, you and Amy Fisher and the rest of the gang.

JACK

Yeah, you say that now, but you'll change your tune after you have kids. Believe me, everybody does.

BARRY

Well, seeing as I'll never have kids, I don't see that being a problem.

JACK

And you're never getting married?

BARRY

No. I'm convinced I'll never have enough interest in any one woman that I'd be willing to give up the joys of bachelorhood. I mean, the grass is always greener.

JACK

Yeah, or thinner or taller, bigger tits . . .

BARRY

Yeah, hopefully . . . hopefully all those things. Which is why, you know, why I can't get over you. I mean . . . you know, Molly is great and everything but, you know, you guys have been together, what, five years? How do you keep it interesting?

JACK

Love.

BARRY

You ever cheat on her?

JACK

No.

BARRY

You never even like, you know, just like thought about it?

JACK

No, not really.

BARRY

You're a better man than me.

JACK

Well, that's not a stretch.

◘INT: JACK AND MOLLY'S BEDROOM. NIGHT

MOLLY and JACK are in bed. JACK is asleep while MOLLY reads. The phone rings and MOLLY answers it.

MOLLY

Hello? . . . Hello?

No one's there. MOLLY shrugs and hangs up.

◘INT: ANN'S BEDROOM. SAME NIGHT

ANN sits on her bed with the phone to her ear. She says nothing. She then hangs up and dials again.

ANN

Hello . . . yeah, may I have the number for the School of Continuing Education at NYU?

◘EXT: NYU CAMPUS. DAY

ANN stands across the street from an NYU school building. She spies JACK walking out of the building. She runs around the block so she can strategically meet up with him. She then turns the corner and is heading JACK'S way. She slows down as they come face-to-face.

JACK

Ann . . .

ANN

Jack . . .

JACK

How are you?

ANN

Good. What are you doing in the city?

JACK

I just got out of class. Those sports management courses I was
telling you about. . . .

ANN

Uh-huh.

JACK

What are you doing?

ANN

Running from meeting to meeting.

JACK

Do . . . you . . . maybe have time for that cup of coffee
now?

ANN

Oh, I'd love to . . . but I'm actually running late. Maybe some
other time?

JACK

Yeah, sure, some other time would be great.

ANN

Okay, some other time then.

JACK

Nice to see you.

ANN

Good to see you too. . . .

They start to walk away from each other. ANN then turns back toward him.

ANN

You know what, how about a walk in the park instead?

JACK

Okay.

ANN grabs JACK by the arm and leads him into the park.

◻EXT: WASHINGTON SQUARE PARK. DAY (CONT)

JACK and ANN walk in the park.

ANN

So . . . you ever cheated on Molly?

JACK

No.

ANN

Never even thought about it?

JACK

No, not really.

ANN

Come on, Jack. None of those little high school girls ever tempted you? God, if I had a teacher that looked like you in high school I would have done everything in my power to get you to keep me after school.

JACK

You're nuts, you know that? Besides, I coach the boys' basketball team.

ANN

Yeah? Well, then I would have become a cheerleader. . . .

◼EXT: PARK BENCH. DAY (CONT)

JACK and ANN sit on a park bench. ANN sits dangerously close to him.

> **ANN**
> So you said you never even thought about cheating on Molly. Does that mean you're thinking about it now?

> **JACK**
> No.

> **ANN**
> You should.

> **JACK**
> Oh, Ann, I don't know. I don't think I could ever do that to Molly.

> **ANN**
> You wouldn't be doing it to Molly. I keep thinking about that night in the car. What would have happened if I just grabbed you and kissed you? Because I know you wanted me to.

ANN pulls JACK closer.

> **ANN**
> Come on, Jack, kiss me.

> **JACK**
> *(jumping up from the bench)*
> Ann, I can't do this, I could never do that to Molly. I love her.

> **ANN**
> I don't want love from you, Jack. I want you.

> **JACK**
> Listen, I got to go.

JACK turns and quickly walks out of the park. ANN sits and watches him go, thinking about what the next plan of attack will be.

◼INT: ATTIC BEDROOM. NIGHT

The lights are out in PATRICK and BARRY'S childhood bedroom. They lie in their beds talking. PATRICK then turns on the light.

BARRY

Do you love her?

PATRICK

Yes, I love her. But that's because we've been together for so long. You know, I have nice memories of those times. But no, I'm not *in* love with her.

BARRY

Are you ready to spend the rest of your life having sex with this one woman? I mean, she'll be the last woman that you get to see completely naked and be allowed to touch. That's something to think about.

PATRICK

I don't know. I thought I'd know when it was time to get married. I envisioned meeting somebody, somewhere, and . . . I thought it was Susan but then it fades, you know; it turns out to be just my imagination. No, what I'm talking about is real, I mean two people mapping out an eternity in a moment. And then we'd sit and have intimate conversation in some dimly lit room, and we'd both feel there was nowhere else in the world we'd want to be in.

BARRY

Jesus Christ, Patrick, I mean, that is very romantic, but there is no fucking chance in hell that's going to happen. Especially to the likes of you.

PATRICK

You don't believe in true love? You don't believe God has someone out there just for you and he allows a lucky few to be fortunate to find one another?

BARRY

How the hell did a fruitcake like you end up as my brother? No,
I do not believe in true love. Okay, but . . . but if there is such a
thing as true love, I'm sure God has nothing to do with it.

PATRICK

You're just afraid. . . . You're just afraid to fall in love, Barry.
Always been afraid of the emotions.

BARRY

Listen, lover boy, all right? We're not on Oprah talking about me
and my emotions, all right? We're talking about you and Susan.

PATRICK

So what do I do? I mean if I move in with her I'm basically
saying yes; yes, I'll eventually marry her. Or do I wait till I find
my true love?

BARRY

I could give two shits about you and your true love, but as far as
Susan goes—she's got to get the ax.

PATRICK

Yeah, yeah, I was thinking that too. But I'm afraid, Barry, I
mean, she is so in love with me I'm afraid she'll do something
crazy like—kill herself.

BARRY

Don't flatter yourself, Patrick, all right? Nobody is killing
themselves over you.

PATRICK

So how do I do it?

BARRY

You came to the right man. It's really quite simple. But the key is
finding the right place. I mean, I like to meet them at work
'cause, you know, there's usually a lot of people around . . .
they're not going to make a big scene, you know, and then you
don't need to worry about driving them home after you just
broke their heart.

PATRICK
Yeah, yeah, that's good thinking.

◘INT: SUSAN'S OFFICE. DAY

*PATRICK sits in SUSAN'S office, a garment center showroom. She is busily
walking back and forth, working.*

PATRICK
What do you mean? I mean, when did this come about?

SUSAN
Look, it's just something I've been thinking about for a long
time, and, you know, the fact that you wouldn't live with me and
the fact that you're not Jewish made it a whole lot easier.

PATRICK
(getting up on his feet)
But why?

SUSAN
Patrick, our relationship has run its course. I think we're
better off going out and finding new people, new experiences,
ideas. . . .

PATRICK
Hey, hey, I don't need any new ideas, all right? I'm confused
enough already. But what about us? I mean, we were going to
get married.

SUSAN
Come on, Patrick, that was just talk, right? We were just kids.
Besides, would you ever be willing to become Jewish? Huh?

PATRICK
(shocked)
Become a Jew!

SUSAN
Yeah.

PATRICK

Convert? Why should I convert? I'm a practicing Catholic, for God's sake. . . .

SUSAN

Oh, yeah.

PATRICK

I go to church once a week. You go to temple, what, once a year? Hey, my religion plays a bigger part in my life than yours does in yours, all right? If anyone should convert, it should be you.

SUSAN

Yeah, but your religion is crazy.

PATRICK

Oh, yeah, yeah. . . .

SUSAN

Listen, I don't even know why I'm talking to you about this right now. Look, it . . . it's over, Patrick, okay? I'm sorry.

SUSAN storms out of the office, leaving PATRICK alone with his thoughts.

PATRICK
(VO)

What does that mean? Experiencing different people? She's going to have sex with other people, that's what that means. This is fine, this is absolutely fine. . . .

◘INT: LONG ISLAND RAIL ROAD. SAME DAY

PATRICK stands in the train staring out the window.

PATRICK
(VO)

This just sucks. . . . That just worked brilliantly. . . . Yeah, Barry, just get them in the office, you know . . . not going to make a scene, lots of people around. . . . She's completely level-headed about the whole thing; I'm on my feet defending my religion, lamely. Unbelievable. . . . I should have to do this? If she were a Catholic girl, believe me you . . .

◼EXT: WEST VILLAGE RESTAURANT. DAY

BARRY and MARTY, Barry's agent, walk out of the restaurant and head down the street.

> MARTY
>
> Okay, I lived up to my end of the bargain, no business during lunch. Lunch is now officially over, so please tell me you're working on something new.

> BARRY
>
> I'm just, I'm—you know, not feeling inspired lately. . . . In fact, I'm not feeling much of anything lately, Marty.

> MARTY
>
> What's wrong this time?

> BARRY
>
> I don't know, I just . . . I can't get into anything I'm writing. I feel like, you know, I'm just going through the motions.

> MARTY
>
> Well, listen, you better find some inspiration soon; for one thing you need the money—and you know what? It's embarrassing; I've got to tell the people in my business that my best young writer lives on Long Island. Writers live in Manhattan, Barry; Joey Buttafuocos live on Long Island, you know what I'm saying?

> BARRY
>
> I got the idea.

> MARTY
>
> You know what you need to do, you need to find another girlfriend with a nice posh Manhattan apartment and set yourself up again. And meanwhile, what happened with Ann? Ann's perfect, and you go blow a relationship with her; what's with that?

BARRY

Yeah, thanks for nothing with Ann; I mean, she was nothing but a pain in the ass.

MARTY

Yeah, well, that pain in the ass told me that Barry takes her out twice and Barry passes out on her twice. You drink too much, man, I've been telling you this for years. You know, this little Hemingway thing you have going is really getting stale.

BARRY

You know what, Marty, blow me.

MARTY

Okay, okay, forget Ann, forget Ann, Ann's old news. Listen, I got a new girl I want to set you up with; she's perfect.

◻EXT: CENTRAL PARK. DAY

A bright and beautiful autumn afternoon. BARRY and AUDREY stroll through the park.

BARRY

You see, you try to fight it but destiny has brought us together.

AUDREY

I think it had more to do with Marty than destiny.

BARRY

Yeah, well, a good agent is supposed to take care of you.

◻EXT: PARK. DAY (CONT)

BARRY and AUDREY sit on a park bench overlooking the pond.

BARRY

So what about . . . you and your fiancé; are you guys happy in my apartment?

AUDREY

He doesn't live in New York.

BARRY

Really? Well, let me ask you a semipersonal question.

AUDREY

Well, you can ask it but I can't guarantee you're going to get an answer.

BARRY

All right, that's fair. Why would you agree to go on a blind date with me if you're already engaged to this . . . Henry the Horse farmer?

AUDREY

Because I'm not happy in that relationship, and I don't want to sell myself short. Besides, Marty said you're a relatively nice guy. . . .

◼ EXT: WEST VILLAGE STREET. SAME DAY

BARRY and AUDREY walk up her stoop. We, of course, recognize it from their first encounter.

AUDREY

Here we are.

BARRY

You know, I still can't forgive you for forcing me into exile out in Long Island.

AUDREY

Oh, come on, it can't be that bad.

BARRY

Yeah, it is that bad. I mean, you're not twenty-five years old and living with your two brothers at home. It's depressing.

AUDREY

You know, Barry, I had a really good time today. I'm kind of surprised. I figured I'd hate you.

BARRY

Ahh, thanks, that's nice. But I actually—I knew that I'd like you from the first time that we met here on the stoop when you stole this apartment from me. I knew . . . you know, well, I guess I . . . I knew that I'd like you.

BARRY slowly moves toward her and kisses her. AUDREY then pulls away.

AUDREY

Barry, I got to go.

BARRY

Yeah . . . no, no, that's . . . that's okay. Ah, but you wanna . . . you wanna get together some other time? Maybe we could go, you know, catch an Audrey Hepburn film at Theater 80 or something?

AUDREY

I . . . I can't, Barry. It's just . . . it wouldn't be fair to Henry.

BARRY

All right. . . . Well, then, some other . . . some other time, then.

AUDREY

Okay.

BARRY

Okay, I'll see you around then. . . . 'Bye.

BARRY *starts off down the street.*

AUDREY

'Bye. . . . Barry! I really liked you. I just can't, I'm sorry.

BARRY
(turning around)
No, that's all right. I mean, you know, you're . . . you're engaged.

AUDREY

For all practical purposes I'm a married woman.

BARRY

Yeah. . . . I'll see you around.

AUDREY

Okay.

BARRY

'Bye.

AUDREY *watches as* BARRY *gives one last look, then walks away.*

◘EXT: MARLBORO ROAD (LONG ISLAND, NY). DAY

A suburban afternoon. As PATRICK walks down his street he spies LESLIE working on her dad's car; then, just as she looks up, he quickly looks away and pretends not to have noticed her.

LESLIE

Hey! Patrick?

PATRICK
(stopping dead in his tracks)

Leslie? Hey.

LESLIE

Oh, God, I thought that was you.

PATRICK

Yeah.

LESLIE

What are you doing?

PATRICK

Well . . . just coming back from the deli actually. . . . I got a
sandwich. What about you? What . . . what are you up to?

LESLIE

Um, just . . . just working on my dad's car.

PATRICK

Oh . . . okay. See you around.

LESLIE

Yeah, okay, 'bye. . . . Patrick! Do . . . do you want a beer with
that sandwich or something?

PATRICK

Okay . . . sure.

▣ EXT: LESLIE'S DRIVEWAY. DAY (CONT)

*LESLIE pulls a beer out of a makeshift cooler and hands it to PATRICK. She
sits down next to him.*

LESLIE

So Patrick, you of all people. . . . God . . . what the hell are you
doing back here?

PATRICK

Oh, well, I had to move back in with Jack, you know. Me and Barry are sharing a crawl space up in the attic.

LESLIE

But I heard that you're . . . that your girlfriend's father was getting you a place in the city.

PATRICK

Yeah, I thought so too, but it doesn't look like that's going to work out.

LESLIE

You got scared, didn't you?

PATRICK

No, I didn't. I mean I was, but . . . you know I wasn't. . . .

LESLIE

Uh-huh.

PATRICK

Her father was also getting me this job, so it just seemed like all of a sudden I had to be this—you know—this real guy with a real life. And I . . . I just was not ready for that. So yeah . . . I got scared. And I just, you know, wanted out of the whole situation.

LESLIE

So what did . . . what did you do?

PATRICK

Well, I didn't have to do anything actually. She broke up with me. Now she's got me thinking that, you know, maybe I do want all those things I . . . I thought I was afraid of.

LESLIE

You know what? It sounds to me like you just want them because you can't have them.

LESLIE lights a cigarette.

LESLIE

So. Why did she break up with you?

PATRICK

See that's . . . that's weird too. She's weird; she wouldn't tell me. Isn't that stupid?

LESLIE

So do you . . . do you still love her?

PATRICK

Not like I think I should. I mean, considering we were going to get married. What about you? I heard you were getting married to Sully?

LESLIE

No. No, I . . . I . . . I couldn't go through with it.

PATRICK

What happened?

LESLIE

I saw the light. . . . It was the morning of my wedding and I was up in the bathroom brushing my teeth and . . . and that's when it hit me; I mean, I suddenly thought, Why?

Cut to flashback:

◘INT: LESLIE'S BATHROOM. MORNING

LESLIE stands in front of the mirror, terrified.

LESLIE

Mom!

Cut back to:

◘EXT: LESLIE'S DRIVEWAY. DAY (CONT)

We pick up PATRICK and LESLIE where we left them.

I thought, Do I really want to spend the rest of my life with James Sullivan?

PATRICK smiles. He knows exactly what she means.

◘EXT: WEST 72ND STREET. DAY

JACK sit in his car across the street from Ann's apartment.

JACK
(VO)
Just take it easy. This is it: one time and then you're done with it.

◘INT: ANN'S APARTMENT. DAY (CONT)

JACK stands in the kitchen, obviously nervous, trying to open a beer. ANN walks over to offer some help.

ANN
It's not a twist-off, Jack.

JACK
I see.

ANN
Don't be so nervous. This is only going to hurt a little bit, Okay? I promise. Come here. . . .

ANN grabs the back of JACK'S head and brings him close. They kiss.

◘INT: ANN'S BEDROOM. EVENING

Candlelit bedroom. ANN and JACK lie in bed, her head on his chest.

ANN
That was nice, wasn't it?

JACK

Mmm, I'll say. Though I have to admit I was a little quick the
first time. But you ought to remember I've been ready to burst
since that day in the park.

ANN

You wanted me that night in the car too, didn't you?

JACK AND ANN

Mm–hm. . . .

ANN

You know you could've had me right then and there. What
made you decide to change your mind?

JACK

I don't know. . . . Something you said about . . . never having sex
with another person for the rest of my life.

ANN

You'll find it's harder to say no the next time.

◘INT: JACK'S CAR. EVENING

JACK *drives home in his car, alone.*

JACK
(VO)

Yeah, but there's not going to be a next time.

◘EXT: MCMULLEN HOUSE. DAY

Winter has arrived. The house and front lawn are covered in snow.

◘INT: MCMULLEN HOUSE. DAY (CONT)

PATRICK *stands in the kitchen, confused and upset.* BARRY *grabs a carton of
milk from the refrigerator.*

PATRICK

So why'd she do it?

BARRY

Patrick, I'm going to tell you for the last time. She doesn't really want to break up with you. She's using this as a method to get back at you. She wants you to come crawling back to her.

PATRICK

So how do I get her back?

BARRY

Why do you even care? I mean, I thought this is what you wanted. I mean, she saved you the trouble of doing the dirty work yourself. You should be happy.

PATRICK

But I miss her.

BARRY

No, you don't.

They head out of the kitchen and through the dining room toward the living room.

PATRICK

Yes, I do.

BARRY

You don't, you just think you do. You're suffering from the "Will I ever get laid again" blues.

PATRICK

No, my friend. I think it's a case of the "You don't know how good you had it till it's gone" syndrome.

BARRY sits down on a couch in the living room, making himself a bowl of cereal. PATRICK follows and sits opposite him.

BARRY

Oh! Tell me what was so great about Susan that you now regret not having it?

PATRICK

Her father was going to get me an apartment and a great new job.

BARRY

Those . . . those are definite pluses. But listen to the advice of your bigger, wiser, and more experienced brother. I have . . . I have a theory: man is like a banana, strong and firm, bright and phallic, and he's protected by his all-important shield. But when a woman comes along, you know, she sees this bright phallic beast and wants it. But she's not happy with it the way it is; she wants to see what's inside. So, she starts to peel away the all-important shield.

BARRY starts to peel the banana.

BARRY

First she wants to see your romantic side. Then she wants to see your passionate side. Then she wants to see your soft, caring, feminine side. And she keeps peeling and peeling until you're left there buck naked, totally exposed, with your balls blowing in the wind.

BARRY picks up a knife and begins cutting the banana.

BARRY

And that's when she gets her knife . . . and she starts to cut away your manhood, piece by piece, until they're having your cock in their corn flakes.

◘EXT: CENTRAL PARK. DAY

SUSAN is jogging in Central Park around the reservoir. PATRICK, expecting to find her here, spots her and begins chasing after her.

PATRICK
(running behind her)
Susan, would you . . . come on, Susan, would you hold up a second? I gotta talk to you. . . . I need to talk to you.

SUSAN

What do you want?

SUSAN stops to walk, and PATRICK catches up.

PATRICK

You broke up with me without an explanation. Now I think I'm entitled to an explanation. I mean, we were going to get married, you know, in case you forgot.

SUSAN

Now tell me the truth. Did you ever really want to get married?

PATRICK

The truth?

SUSAN

Yeah, remember: "Thou shalt not lie."

PATRICK

The truth? The truth is no, but that's because . . . that's before I realized how much I need you in my life.

SUSAN

You don't need me, you just think you do.

PATRICK

What is the difference? This is where I am.

SUSAN

Look, I just don't think it would be healthy for either one of us to stay together right now, okay? I mean especially considering the current situation.

PATRICK

Whoa, whoa, whoa, whoa . . . what current situation?

SUSAN

Look, Patrick, I really don't feel like talking to you right now, okay? Will you just . . . leave me alone!

SUSAN takes off again, leaving PATRICK standing there.

■EXT: CENTRAL PARK. DAY

A sunny New York winter afternoon. BARRY and AUDREY walk along Bethesda Fountain.

> BARRY
> I can't believe you liked that movie.

> AUDREY
> It was fun.

> BARRY
> It was crap. You know what, you're going to have to read my new script.

> AUDREY
> Why? What's it about?

> BARRY
> It's about this guy and his quest for true love.

> AUDREY
> And does he find it?

> BARRY
> Well, of course not.

■EXT: CENTRAL PARK. DAY (CONT)

BARRY and AUDREY sit on a park bench.

> AUDREY
> You've never been in love, have you?

> BARRY
> Well . . .

> AUDREY
> You haven't, have you? Do you love anybody?

BARRY

Well, yeah, I mean, you know, I love—you know I guess . . . I
guess I . . . I love my brothers. . . . I love . . . I love my mother. In
fact, yeah, I love my mother very much.

AUDREY

How sweet. And does your mommy live with you and your
brothers too?

BARRY

No, no, my mommy actually . . . moved back to Ireland a couple
of years ago.

AUDREY

Ireland, why?

BARRY

Well, this—you'll love this story; this is right up your alley. I
guess it was about five years ago. My dad finally died . . . we
were all very excited about that . . . and right after his funeral my
mom pulls me aside and she says to me . . .

Cut to flashback:

◘EXT: CALVARY GRAVEYARD. DAY

*MRS. McMULLEN and BARRY stand in the graveyard where we found
them in the first scene.*

MRS. McMULLEN

Promise me you won't make the same mistake I made.

BARRY

Yeah, yeah, I promise.

Cut to:

◘EXT: CENTRAL PARK. DAY (CONT)

BARRY and AUDREY sit on the bench where we left them.

BARRY

Yeah, she just she took off that night.

AUDREY

Why would she marry your dad if she didn't love him?

BARRY

'Cause she's Catholic, I guess. I mean, she fell in love with this
guy, Finbar O'Shaughnessy, whom I'm named after, although
my dad didn't know that, but she was already pregnant with
my dad's baby, which is my brother Jack. So you know, like
any good Catholic girl would, she got married. They ended
up moving to America, and she had to wait thirty-five years
until the old man, you know, died, so that she could go back
to Ireland and finally be, you know, reunited with her true
love.

AUDREY

Wow! Now that is a great love story. With a mom like that,
you'd think you'd be a hopeless romantic instead of a loveless
pessimist.

BARRY

Hey, I like being a pessimist, you know? It makes it easier to deal
with my inevitable failure.

*They get up off the bench and head out of the park, continuing their
conversation.*

AUDREY

So where is your mom now?

BARRY

Well, she and O'Shaughnessy live in Dublin. He's a champion
fiddle player, so whenever they come to New York to perform,
you know, the whole band comes out to the house and my
mom cooks her famous corned beef and cabbage.

AUDREY
(dropping a hint)
Mmm, I love corned beef and cabbage.

> BARRY
> *(laughing)*

Yeah, well, we'll see.

◘INT: AUDREY'S APARTMENT. DAY

BARRY and AUDREY sit side by side on the couch. They both appear uncomfortable. BARRY leans forward with a beer in his hand.

> BARRY
> *(VO)*

Okay, Finbar, just lean back and do it. . . . Come on, you coward, just do it.

BARRY leans back and looks at AUDREY. She moves toward him and they kiss. AUDREY then pulls away.

> AUDREY

Barry, I have a confession to make.

> BARRY
> *(concerned)*

Well, what is it?

> AUDREY

Promise me you won't be mad.

> BARRY

Well, how can if I'll be mad if I don't know what it is you're going to confess?

> AUDREY

I'm not engaged. Henry has asked me a thousand times, but I just cannot bring myself to say yes.

> BARRY

Really? . . . I mean, that's great. I mean, it's too bad for Henry, but he's not really high on my list of concerns.

> AUDREY

Are you happy?

BARRY

Fucking-A, I'm happy. That's great. Would you mind . . . if I
kissed you again?

AUDREY

Think you can handle it?

BARRY

I think I can handle it.

◘INT: NYC CAB. SAME DAY

BARRY sits in the backseat of a cab on his way home from Audrey's.

BARRY
(VO)
Yeah, right. There's no way you can handle this.

◘INT: JACK AND MOLLY'S BEDROOM. NIGHT

MOLLY sits at her desk, grading papers. JACK walks in.

JACK

Hey, doll, how are the papers coming?

MOLLY

Hey, good. You coming to bed soon? I miss you. I feel like we
never get to see each other anymore.

JACK

Yeah, I know, but I'm going to hit the sack. I'm kind of tired.

MOLLY

I think I'll finish grading these in the morning.

MOLLY gets up from the desk and approaches JACK.

JACK

Why? You're better off getting them done tonight.

MOLLY

Well, I was . . . I was thinking you might be interested in doing a little something you haven't done in a while.

JACK

I thought you got embarrassed by that.

MOLLY

Well, maybe I'm feeling a little less inhibited tonight.

JACK

Oh, really?

MOLLY

Yeah.

JACK

I'm sorry, honey, I'm not in the mood. I'm tired.

JACK walks away from her to the other side of the bedroom.

MOLLY

Wow! Oh, I remember the days when you used to say, "I don't get these guys who say they're too tired for sex. I'll never be too tired for sex."

JACK
(yelling)
Oh, come on, Molly, the one night that I'm not in the mood you're going to break my balls about it? How about all the nights you haven't been in the mood, huh?

MOLLY

I'm sorry, Jack. I was just kidding. I guess I thought it might be fun, that's all.

MOLLY exits the room. JACK tries to call out to her as she leaves.

JACK

Look, I'm . . . I'm sorry I yelled at you, hon. I've just been feeling kind of weird these days, I don't know.

◼INT: KITCHEN. MORNING

MOLLY sits at the kitchen table, chopping vegetables. BARRY enters and grabs a beer from the fridge.

> MOLLY
>
> So Barry, I think that if you like her that much you should just call her up and ask her out again.

> BARRY
>
> Yeah, but she's not Irish.

> MOLLY
>
> Well, then, you've got to forget about it.

> BARRY
>
> I don't know if I can. I mean, she's the most beautiful woman that I have ever been in contact with. I mean, she is gorgeous. She's proof that God is indeed a man.

> MOLLY
>
> You are in love!

> BARRY
>
> Don't talk to me about love. What did I say? All I said was she's beautiful; I said nothing about love.

> MOLLY
>
> No, no, no, no, no, you're in love. Trust me, I know when someone is or isn't in love.

JACK comes walking into the kitchen from the side door.

> JACK
>
> Hey, doll.

> MOLLY
>
> Hey, honey.

JACK
(to BARRY)
What, are you drinking all my frigging beers?

BARRY
I'm having one beer, give me a fucking break.

JACK
It's not even noon and you're drinking already.

BARRY
When did you all of a sudden become my mother, huh? I can't drink beer anymore? You gonna tell me when I can and can't drink, huh, Big Jack?

JACK
Look, I'm not your mother but I'm going to go out for a jog, and when I come back I want a couple of beers in the house, okay?

MOLLY
You're going out for a run, Jack?

JACK
Yeah, I'm going to try to work off these love handles.

BARRY
Yeah, well, you could use it, lard–ass, huh?

MOLLY
Hey, you want some company? I'd love to go for a run.

JACK
No, that's all right. I'm just going to hop out for a quickie. I'll be back.

JACK heads out of the house.

BARRY
(calling after him)
Yeah, have a few more doughnuts while you're at it, fat boy.

MOLLY *watches* JACK *go and seems to become suspicious of Jack's behavior. She turns to* BARRY.

> MOLLY
>
> Do you think Jack would ever have an affair?

> BARRY
>
> Jack? No way, no how. I mean, he loves you; you were the answer to that guy's dreams. Besides, do you think there's somebody out there better than you?

> MOLLY
>
> Nah, I don't know. I don't know, he just seems kind of distant lately. Maybe I'm bugging him too much about having a baby.

◘INT: ANN'S APARTMENT. DAY

ANN *is at the sink.* JACK *slides up behind her and kisses her neck.*

> JACK
>
> God, you know, a minute doesn't pass by where I don't think about making love to you.

> ANN
>
> Easy there, coach, there'll be no lovemaking going on here.

ANN *turns around into his arms.*

> JACK
>
> It's a figure of speech.

> ANN
>
> Yeah, well, next time try another figure, like, "Do it." Like I would say, I thought you were feeling too guilty to "do it" with me.

> JACK
>
> All right, how about, I can do it now . . . and deal with the guilt of having done it later.

ANN

Very good.

They begin to kiss.

◘EXT: McMULLEN HOUSE. MORNING

It is early morning and PATRICK, dressed only in boxer shorts, peeks out the front door. He quickly runs out and down the stoop, grabs the newspaper off the lawn, and runs back inside the house, straight up to the bathroom.

◘INT: HALLWAY. SAME MORNING

JACK walks down the hall and knocks on the bathroom door.

JACK

Hey, who's in there?

PATRICK
(OS)

It's me. Hey, I'm going to the bathroom!

JACK

I've got to come in there, I've got to get something.

JACK just walks in on PATRICK.

◘INT: BATHROOM. DAY (CONT)

JACK

Oh, Jesus, how about a mercy flush, huh?

PATRICK
(OS)

What the hell do you expect it to smell like? Hey, I'm going to the bathroom here, do you mind?

JACK

Yeah, well, you ought to be going to see a doctor. Either that or I'll get Molly to change butchers.

PATRICK
(OS)

Very funny.

JACK

Patrick, Patrick. Listen, I got to talk to you.

JACK *closes the bathroom door and sits on the edge of the tub opposite*
PATRICK, *who, we see now, is sitting on the bowl.*

PATRICK

What is it?

JACK

Let me ask you something. You're Mr. Ten Commandments, right? How bad a sin is adultery?

PATRICK

You're cheating on Molly?

JACK

No, I'm not cheating on Molly. But, you know, I am starting to get feelings for other women now, and I was just wondering, if I did give in to temptation, then how bad a sin is that?

PATRICK

It's horrible. Jack, you can't do it. First of all, it's a big-time sin. Second of all, I love Molly. You can't do something like that to her. Why would you ever want to cheat on Molly? She's the greatest.

JACK

Yeah, I know, I know, but, you know, sometimes you need a change in your life. I mean, I don't want to do anything, but, you know, Molly and I have been together almost five frigging years.

PATRICK

I'm stunned. I can't believe this. You're actually considering sticking your penis into another woman?

JACK

Well, that's usually how it works.

PATRICK

Jack, you've got to fight it. It's just not fair to Molly. Inasmuch as we don't believe in it, I would say, get a divorce before you do something like that.

(beat)

Who is she?

JACK

It's nobody, really, I'm just thinking.

PATRICK

Come on, Jack, she's somebody.

JACK

Look, she's nobody, okay? And don't say a word to Barry either, all right?

PATRICK

Of course not.

JACK

And listen, don't forget to wipe yourself, all right?

JACK stands and exits the bathroom.

◾EXT: LESLIE'S FRONT PORCH. DAY

PATRICK and LESLIE are hanging out on a sunny afternoon.

PATRICK

I mean, how do you know whether the one you're with is or is not your true soul mate? And then, what if you let them go and never find anybody to replace them?

LESLIE

Yeah, but I think you're better off being alone than . . . than being with somebody that isn't your true soul mate. Anyway, sometimes you've just got to take chances.

PATRICK

You know . . . speaking of chances and not taking them . . . you know how we . . . I always sort of wanted to ask you out in high school. But, you know, you were always with Sully and so . . . I never did.

LESLIE

Oh, yeah?

PATRICK

Yeah.

LESLIE

Well, you should have.

LESLIE walks into the house, leaving PATRICK pleasantly surprised. She quickly reappears with two beers.

PATRICK

So what are you going to do now?

LESLIE

Well, after I canceled my wedding I reevaluated my whole life and I became a vegetarian, a pro-choice activist, and . . . I abandoned Catholicism.

PATRICK

Really? But I remember a summer you were going away to that convent, you were going to be a nun! What is this? Why would you abandon Catholicism?

LESLIE

Because I tried to figure out why I said yes to James and that's when it hit me . . . I mean . . . I thought I had to get married, you know. What's a single Catholic girl going to do if she doesn't get married? I can't have premarital sex, but if I do have sex I can't use birth control, but if I don't use birth control and I get pregnant, I can't have an abortion, so what's a girl supposed to do while she's waiting around for Prince Charming to show up? I mean, Christ, I can't even masturbate.

PATRICK

Tell me about that one. If I masturbated as much as I wanted to,
I swear to God I would live in a constant state of guilt. Not to
mention hospitalization.

LESLIE

I know, it's crazy; you can't be Catholic and have a healthy sex
life.

PATRICK

Unless you find your true love.

LESLIE

Well, yeah okay then . . . then and only then.

They smile at each other and quickly look away, embarrassed.

◼EXT: WEST 81ST STREET. DAY

*PATRICK is waiting on the street outside SUSAN'S apartment. She exits, and
he walks with her down the street. SUSAN walks quickly to keep ahead of
PATRICK, whom she obviously doesn't want to talk to.*

PATRICK

I need to talk to you.

SUSAN

What do you want?

PATRICK

Susan, I think I deserve an explanation.

SUSAN

You think you deserve an explanation?

PATRICK

Yes.

SUSAN stops dead in her tracks.

SUSAN

All right. Well, this is going to knock your Catholic socks right off! The current situation is, I'm pregnant.

PATRICK

You're pregnant with my baby?

SUSAN

I've only been with you, Patrick.

PATRICK

Jesus, Mary, and Joseph. You're pregnant with my baby? How did this happen? We . . . I thought we were taking every precaution. I even wore two rubbers at once. I thought you were on the pill; I thought you were right on top of it.

SUSAN

I was. I still am. The pill is only ninety-nine percent effective. Well, we fell into that one percent.

PATRICK

So why would you want to break up with me now? I mean, under the current circumstances, I would figure you would want to get married.

SUSAN

Hello, Patrick, I'm twenty-one years old. I don't want to have a baby, and if we got married you'd want me to have the baby, right?

PATRICK

Of course. Why, what else would you do?

SUSAN

I'm going to have an abortion.

PATRICK

An abortion? You can't have an abortion. That's against everything I believe in!

SUSAN

Well, the last time I checked, the baby was in my stomach and not in yours, so I'll make the decision.

PATRICK

That child is half mine.

SUSAN

Not anymore. Listen, Patrick, I . . . I've got to go. . . . I'm sorry. I knew you wouldn't agree with my decision, so that's why I did what I did.

SUSAN walks away, leaving PATRICK standing there.

◻EXT: ST. JOSEPH'S CHURCH. DAY

PATRICK, obviously racked with guilt, exits the church.

PATRICK
(VO)

I'm going to hell.

◻EXT: JACK AND MOLLY'S BACKYARD. DAY

PATRICK and JACK are in the yard raking leaves.

PATRICK

Jack, do you believe in hell?

JACK

Hey, I haven't done anything yet, okay?

PATRICK

I'm not talking about you anyway. I think I'm going to hell.

JACK

Oh, Jesus Christ, altar boy, why are you going to hell this time?

PATRICK

First of all, I had sex with Susan out of wedlock.

JACK

Big deal.

PATRICK

Now I find out, the reason she breaks up with me is because she's pregnant. And now—now she's having an abortion.

JACK

Oh, you're shitting me. You got her pregnant?

PATRICK

Yeah.

JACK

Well, just be thankful she's getting an abortion.

◘INT: LESLIE'S KITCHEN. DAY

PATRICK and LESLIE hang out in her kitchen, grilling some hot dogs.

LESLIE

Relax, you're not going to hell.

PATRICK

She's having an abortion. Can you believe that?

LESLIE

Good. Good for her.

PATRICK

Good for her? Well, what about me? I am a Catholic. My life is over, I'm going to hell.

LESLIE

You know what you should do? You should come to California with me.

PATRICK

Oh, solution of solutions. When are you going to California?

LESLIE

As soon as I can get enough money. I've already got two thousand saved, and all I need is another two grand and I can buy this beautiful cherry 1970 Chevelle I've had my eye on. As soon as I can get the money, I'm gone.

PATRICK

Drive cross-country. Yeah, that sounds great. I could use some adventure like that.

LESLIE

If you can come up with two thousand dollars, we can leave tomorrow.

Leslie grabs a hot dog off the grill and starts to chow it down.

PATRICK

Sure you could stand to be alone with me all that time? It's a pretty long trip.

LESLIE

Well, I asked you, didn't I?

PATRICK

Yeah.
(*pointing to Leslie's hot dog*)
What's this? I thought you said you didn't eat meat.

LESLIE

Only on Fridays.

◘INT: JACK'S CAR. DAY

A gray late-winter afternoon. JACK and ANN sit parked outside her apartment.

ANN

What's wrong with you? You've been acting strange all day.

JACK

I just don't feel that this is right. For Christ's sake, don't you have any guilt at all?

ANN

Don't get so high and mighty on yourself, Jack. You know, in case you haven't noticed, you're the one who has been calling me lately. Not the other way around.

JACK

Look, I'm sorry. This whole thing just got my head a little bit
screwed up right now.

ANN

You're having an affair. It's not a big fucking deal.

JACK

Well, it is to me. I mean, I don't like what I'm doing. I don't
want to hurt Molly. I love her.

ANN

Get over yourself, Jack. If you loved Molly so much you
wouldn't be running into the city, jumping into my bed every
chance you get.
(beat)
Great. You know what? Do me a favor. I don't want to be part
of your confusion; don't bother coming up. Call me when you
get a grip.

ANN gets out of the car and slams the door.

JACK

Damn!

◘EXT: McMULLEN HOUSE. SAME DAY

*PATRICK is taking the garbage out to the curb as JACK pulls up and gets out
of his car. PATRICK knows where JACK has just been, and it shows on his
face.*

JACK

What? You got a problem?

PATRICK

You did it.

JACK

I did nothing. Okay?

PATRICK

Oh, Jack, I told you not to do it. That is a big-time sin. Not to mention what effect it's going to have on Molly, your marriage—

JACK

Yeah? Well, you better not say a word to Molly, or to Barry either, you hear me?

PATRICK

What the . . . Jack, I wouldn't think of it. Jesus! It was that Ann, that Barry used to see, wasn't it?

JACK

Look, I fucked up, okay? I mean, I know I didn't do the right thing, but I felt like I had to do it anyway. Look, I love Molly, you know, I really do but—I mean, who says you've got to be one hundred percent faithful to your wife anyway? It just isn't natural.

PATRICK

God said.

JACK

Well, fuck God, all right? Why should I spend all my time and waste all my faith in something I have absolutely no proof ever even existed? Patrick, I'm a man, I had a certain urge, and I acted on it. I don't see that as being such a big deal.

PATRICK
(horrified)
Fuck God? Well, that's a big deal for Molly, don't you think? You're going to have to make a choice, Jack. You can't go on this way.

JACK

Well, first of all, Patrick, this isn't your problem to worry about, all right? Second of all, I know what I got to do.

PATRICK

Hey, Jack, I really hope you do, man.

JACK walks up the stoop and enters the house.

■EXT: LONG ISLAND RAIL ROAD PLATFORM. DAY

Spring is here. BARRY stands on the platform looking for the train. AUDREY sits on the platform enjoying the sun.

> BARRY
>
> Where the hell is this train already?

> AUDREY
>
> Hey, Fin, come sit by me.

BARRY sits down next to her on the steps.

> AUDREY
> *(showing off her new ring)*
>
> Hey, want to see my new ring?

> BARRY
>
> Yeah, I've seen the ring.

> AUDREY
>
> Tell me what it's called again.

> BARRY
>
> It's called a Claddah ring. And the hands represent friendship and the crown on top represents loyalty.

> AUDREY
>
> What about the heart?

> BARRY
>
> The heart represents, you know, like a . . . deeper sort of friendship. You know, like a . . . you know, just like a deep friendship.

> AUDREY
>
> Friendship?

> BARRY
>
> Yeah.

AUDREY

Not love?

BARRY

No. I mean . . . I guess the heart could be looked at as love. But
enough about the goddamn ring. Tell me, did you read the script
yet or what?

AUDREY

How could I have read it? I just got it this afternoon.

BARRY

You're going to read it tonight though?

AUDREY

I promise, by the time I go to sleep tonight it will have been read.

BARRY

Promise?

AUDREY

Barry, I'll read the script.

◼ INT: JACK AND MOLLY'S LIVING ROOM. DAY

PATRICK rushes into the living room to talk to JACK and MOLLY.

MOLLY

Patrick, what happened?

JACK

Let me guess. You're not going to California anymore?

PATRICK

Can someone lend me ten bucks for the train? Please.

JACK

She wants you back?

PATRICK

She wants me back.

JACK

What about the baby?

PATRICK

She had a miscarriage.

MOLLY

Oh, my God.

JACK

Jeez, talk about the luck of the Irish.

MOLLY

Jack!

PATRICK

Yeah, yeah, it's great, isn't it. Listen, can I have the ten bucks? I'm going to miss my train.

JACK

Yeah, sure.

JACK hands PATRICK the money; he runs out of the house. MOLLY looks at JACK and shakes her head. She turns and heads up the stairs in disgust.

◘INT: LONG ISLAND RAIL ROAD. SAME DAY

PATRICK anxiously sits on the train.

◘INT: SUSAN'S OFFICE. SAME DAY

PATRICK sits listening in the office. Gaudy sweaters cover the walls. SUSAN is busily walking around the room, talking a mile a minute.

SUSAN

Hey. So guess what? I spoke to Daddy, and he said he is going to buy you that one-bedroom on the first floor, so that way we can at least be in the same building, and then after we're married we can move into that beautiful two-bedroom on the fourth floor.

PATRICK
He's going to pay for me to live in the same building with
you?

SUSAN
Of course. Well, you know, he loves me and I love you so he
loves you. And he wants you to start off working in the sales
department. He feels like it's the best way for you to learn the
business.

PATRICK
Susan, I don't know if I can work for your father.

SUSAN
Why not, hon?

PATRICK
Because he's done so much for me already—

SUSAN
No! Don't be silly. It's going to be great, Patrick. We're going to
move in; everything will be fine. And you know what I was
thinking. . . .

SUSAN *continues to run around the office, talking nonstop. As PATRICK*
stands up and crosses to a sweater rack, SUSAN'S voice drops out and we hear
PATRICK'S voiceover.

PATRICK
(VO)
Oh, God, I thank you; I thank you for letting her have that
miscarriage. But just look at these sweaters.

SUSAN
Patrick, are you listening to me?

PATRICK
Yeah.

SUSAN
What's wrong?

PATRICK

Listen, Susan, I'm sorry, but I don't want to work in the garment district, okay? And I don't want to live in the same building with you.

SUSAN

Why not?

PATRICK

Because I want to move on with my life. And because I don't love you anymore.

SUSAN

You don't love me anymore?

SUSAN is taken aback. Then what he said hits her.

SUSAN

Get out of here. Get out! Get out of here, Patrick, leave!

PATRICK starts to backpedal out of the office.

SUSAN

Patrick, leave, get out! Come on, leave me alone!

PATRICK

Okay. Fine.

PATRICK turns and exits.

◘EXT: CITY STREET. SAME DAY

PATRICK runs to a pay phone and tries to make a call.

◘EXT: LONG ISLAND RAIL ROAD PLATFORM. SAME DAY

The train pulls into the station, and as soon as the doors open PATRICK is the first to exit the train. He takes off running down the platform.

◼EXT: SUBURBAN STREET. SAME DAY

A short montage of PATRICK running down the streets of his town until he finally spots LESLIE sitting on her car in front of her house. He approaches her, out of breath.

PATRICK

Leslie! I need to talk to you.

LESLIE

Patrick! What's up?

PATRICK

You were serious when you asked me to come to California with you, right?

LESLIE

Yeah.

PATRICK

Well, how do you feel about me?

LESLIE

What do you mean?

PATRICK

Well, I mean, how do you feel about me? I mean . . . remember yesterday when we were talking about finding your true love and how great that must be?

LESLIE

Yeah.

PATRICK

Well, I think I've got a pretty good idea.

LESLIE

Um . . .

PATRICK

I don't mean that—I mean, I do mean that, but . . . what I mean is—I want to go to California with you.

LESLIE

Well, good. I want you to come to California with me.

PATRICK

I know, I know, you said that, but . . . how do you feel about me?

LESLIE

What do you mean? I mean, do . . . do you . . . do you mean, do
I—

PATRICK

No, no, no, you don't have to say the words. I mean I . . . I just
want to know if you have . . . if you have any idea . . . I mean,
any feeling in that way . . . that just . . . something.

LESLIE

Yeah.

PATRICK

Yeah?

LESLIE

Yeah . . . yeah.

PATRICK

Yeah?

LESLIE

Yeah. But you know I'm not Catholic anymore.

PATRICK

Yeah, yeah, I know that. I thought about that and I don't give a
shit.

◼ INT: McMULLEN BASEMENT. DAY

*MOLLY is doing laundry in the basement. As she goes through the pockets of a
pair of JACK'S pants, she finds condoms in one of the pockets. Her suspicions
have been confirmed.*

◻EXT: JACK AND MOLLY'S BACKYARD. DAY

MOLLY sits on a lawn chair in the backyard, holding the condoms. JACK walks out of the back door into the yard.

> JACK
>
> What are you doing out here all by your lonesome?

> MOLLY
>
> Just thinking.

JACK sits on a chair behind her.

> JACK
>
> It's awful quiet without those guys around here, huh?

MOLLY doesn't respond. JACK knows something's up.

> JACK
>
> Hey, listen, I was thinking maybe we should take a vacation
> sometime soon, someplace warm. What do you think?

> MOLLY
>
> I don't want to run away from here to work out our problems,
> Jack. This is our home. If you feel like you've got something
> you've got to work out, let's just do it right here.

MOLLY stands and walks to the fence. JACK follows.

> JACK
>
> Problems? What are you talking about?

> MOLLY
>
> What problems do we have, Jack? Are you that far removed from
> this relationship?

> JACK
>
> Listen, I realize I've been a little distant lately. . . .

MOLLY

Distant, Jack? We haven't had sex in months.

JACK

Well, why don't you scream it a little louder so that the whole fucking neighborhood can hear you? Listen, I'm going through a weird period in my life right now. I mean it seems like it was just yesterday that I was a kid in high school, and all of a sudden I'm thirty-three years old and thinking about starting a family.

MOLLY

Oh, come on, Jack, you're just about fifteen years too early to be having your midlife crisis.

JACK

I don't want to become like my father, a miserable fucking prick who isn't there for you, isn't there for the kids. The thing is . . . I don't even know if I can be a good father.

MOLLY

That's bullshit, Jack, and you know it. Don't use kids as your excuse. And the way your father was is the exact reason why you would be a great father. You know that I would never ask you for a divorce. And I'm willing to wait for you to do whatever it is you feel like you've got to do, but, you know, out of respect for me and out of respect for what we've had and for what we still could have . . . if you feel like you've got to go do something . . .

JACK

What the hell are you talking about?

MOLLY

I'm not a fool, Jack.

MOLLY storms off into the house.

◘EXT: CALVARY GRAVEYARD. DAY

JACK is standing alone in the cemetery at his father's grave.

JACK
(VO)

Dad, I just stopped by today to say good-bye and let you know
that I'm not going to be the kind of man that you were. Happy
St. Patrick's Day.

JACK pulls out a flask and pours the drink onto the grave.

◻INT: ATTIC BEDROOM. NIGHT

*BARRY walks up the stairs into the attic. PATRICK is sitting on his bed,
reading.*

BARRY

Hey, Pat.

PATRICK

Hey.

BARRY

Can . . . can you talk?

PATRICK

Yeah, what's up?

BARRY

I got a problem.

PATRICK

What is it?

BARRY

It's Audrey. Marty thinks something really big is going to happen
with the script. He thinks they're going to want me to come out
to California; he said, you know, some really big-name actresses
are interested in the lead.

PATRICK

Okay, so where's the problem?

BARRY

What am I going to do about Audrey? I mean, I promised her the part.

PATRICK

Do you love her?

BARRY

I might.

PATRICK

So now you finally get a decent script in your hands and you're going to throw your inspiration right out the window?

BARRY
(almost to himself)

Just when things are starting to happen for me, I've got to go and fall in love.

◘EXT: CENTRAL PARK. DAY

A beautiful spring afternoon. AUDREY and BARRY stand by the side of the lake.

IAN TONG

AUDREY

Is something bothering you? You've been very distant the last few days.

BARRY

No I just . . . I got a lot on my mind, that's all.

AUDREY

I spoke to Henry last night. He wants me to come back to Virginia.

BARRY

What are you going to do?

AUDREY

I don't know. What do you want me to do?

BARRY

I don't want you to go back to Virginia and marry Henry.

AUDREY

But you don't know if you want to continue this relationship either, do you?

BARRY

Well, I don't know what I want to do about anything right now, Audrey.

AUDREY

You mean you don't know what you want to do about us.

BARRY

I mean everything happened so quickly for us. . . . I mean . . . it took me by surprise, I guess. I thought we'd go out for a few drinks, have few laughs. . . .

AUDREY

And instead?

BARRY

And instead we got . . . you know . . . we got really serious.

AUDREY

And that scares you?

BARRY

Yeah, that fucking scares me.

AUDREY

So . . . what do we do now?

BARRY

I don't know. What do you think we should do?

AUDREY

I don't know. I just want to be with you, Barry.

BARRY

I don't know if that's possible anymore, Audrey. I just need some
time to figure some things out. Maybe we should spend some
time away from one another and see how that works out.

AUDREY

Well, I'll wait for you for a little while, but I can't wait forever.

She waits for BARRY to say something. He doesn't.

AUDREY

Okay, I'm going to go home now. I'll see you around then?

*BARRY nods but continues to stare at the ground, afraid to look at her. AUDREY
shakes her head and heads up the path, leaving BARRY by the edge of the lake.*

◼EXT: McMULLEN HOUSE. DAY

PATRICK and BARRY are carrying groceries into the house.

PATRICK

It's Palm Sunday. I went to church.

BARRY

Congratulations.

PATRICK

So what did you give up for Lent?

BARRY

I'm giving up resolutions this year.

PATRICK

Convenient. You know, you made a mistake, Barry. She doesn't
want a husband, man, she wants you.

BARRY

That's the same thing, as far as I'm concerned.

PATRICK

No, it's not the same thing; it's not. You get one chance in this
life, if you're lucky.

BARRY

Yeah, I'm sure there'll be others, Pat.

PATRICK

No, there won't. Just think about Mom.

BARRY

Don't start with that shit again.

PATRICK

You know, Barry, if you just took one second to look at yourself,
you might discover what you truly want.

BARRY

Oh, yeah, and what's that? Why don't you fucking tell me what
that is, huh?

PATRICK

To ask her to marry you.

◘INT: AUDREY'S APARTMENT. NIGHT

AUDREY, alone, reads in her apartment. She is clearly upset.

◘INT: McMULLEN KITCHEN. NIGHT

BARRY sits alone at the kitchen table. It is obvious that he has a lot on his mind; namely, AUDREY.

◘INT: McMULLEN GARAGE. DAY

A rainy day. MOLLY sits on a crate in the garage going through a box filled with books. JACK walks into the garage.

> JACK
>
> Oh, I didn't know that you where home.

> MOLLY
>
> Yeah, I'm trying to find some Fitzgerald stories for class tomorrow. Remember this?

MOLLY hands a paperback to JACK. He flips through it.

> JACK
>
> Yeah.

An uncomfortable silence.

> JACK
>
> Think we've lost the romance from our marriage?

> MOLLY
>
> No, I just don't think you're interested anymore. You know, I think that sometimes in our lives when we start to grow accustomed to things we start to not see them anymore, you know, or to kind of look past them. And we sort of have a tendency to . . . I don't know, want something new and different, you know, because we feel like that's going to fulfill whatever it is . . . that seems to be missing in our lives. But it doesn't. And so I think that we just need to look back at what we do have in our lives and try to remember what it was that brought us there in the first place. You know? So . . . so why did you do it, Jack? I mean, what didn't I do for you?

JACK

What are you talking about?

MOLLY

I know that you've been seeing someone else, okay? I found
your rubbers.

JACK

What rubbers?

MOLLY

Oh, come on, Jack, I don't want to have to fight for you. Why
can't you just be a man and admit it?

JACK

What do you want me to say?

MOLLY

When did you become such a fucking coward? I want you to
tell me the truth, okay. Did you do it?

JACK looks up and nods.

MOLLY

Why, Jack, why?

JACK

Honey, I am so sorry. I just want to be with you again.

MOLLY

I don't know, you know? I think it's going to take a long time.

JACK

I know. I know.

MOLLY

Is it over?

JACK

Yes, it's over.

MOLLY

Did you love her?

JACK

No.

◘ INT: LESLIE'S BEDROOM. DAY

PATRICK and LESLIE are in bed together, under the sheets. We don't know who it is until they both emerge from underneath the covers on opposite ends of the bed. PATRICK rubs his jaw.

PATRICK

Jesus Christ!

LESLIE

What's wrong?

PATRICK

I don't know.

LESLIE

Are you okay?

PATRICK

Yeah. I think so. I don't know. Did you?

LESLIE

Yeah, yeah, why can't you?

PATRICK

Whoa, whoa, I can. . . . I'm just a little nervous.

LESLIE

Oh, why? What's wrong?

PATRICK

Listen, there's something I've got to tell you.

LESLIE

What is it?

PATRICK

I got the money.

LESLIE

What money?

PATRICK

The two thousand. My brother wrote me the check.

LESLIE

For the car? Oh, my God, you mean we're going?

PATRICK

As soon as you want.

LESLIE

Ohhhhh, I love you!

She reaches for him and kisses him.

PATRICK

Hey, that's just the kind of guy I am.

◘EXT: McMULLEN HOUSE. DAY

PATRICK steps out of the house to deliver a few beers to JACK and BARRY, who are sitting on the side stoop. PATRICK sits with them.

JACK

Did you go to Dublin for these?

BARRY

Yeah. How's the jelly roll, huh?

PATRICK

I can't believe this is it. Told you I'd be out of here by Easter.

BARRY

I can't believe you're actually going through with this. I mean, I didn't think you had balls big enough for a stunt like this.

JACK
Really.

PATRICK
It's got nothing to do with my balls, man. You know, it's got everything to do with my heart. You know, when you find your true companion—

JACK
Stop. Stop right there, please.

BARRY
Jesus, yeah, yeah. I mean I think we've all had enough true-love talk to last us a fucking lifetime.

JACK
Speaking of which, you decided what you're going to do with Audrey?

BARRY
No. No, I don't know.

PATRICK
I don't know about you guys, but these past few months have really been special for me. I mean, living under the same roof again. I mean, it really felt like a home—you know, like a family.

BARRY
Yeah, despite the fact that there wasn't a psychotic drunk screaming for beers and beating the shit out of us every day.

JACK
Yeah, what was all that crazy shit he used to say to us when he had half a bag on?

PATRICK
Shut your fucking mouth when you're talking to me, pal.

JACK
Yeah, and the time I came home in my new varsity jacket and I was really proud of it and I was, like, "Hey, Dad, what do you

think of my new jacket?" And he was, like, "Why don't you get another one in blue and burn the both of them?"

                              BARRY
I remember he always used to say to me, "Hey, shit-for-brains, the only thing I want to hear out of you . . . is nothing." Fucking prick.

                              PATRICK
Yeah, prick is right.

                              JACK
So what time are you and Leslie leaving?

                              PATRICK
Oh, well . . . she wants to get on the road bright and early so she's figured five o'clock, five A.M.

                              JACK
That's early.

                              PATRICK
Yeah. You guys be up for a good-bye at that time?

                              JACK
I don't think so.

                              BARRY
I think you could bet your ass that I'm not going to be up at five in the morning.

                              PATRICK
Well, I guess this is it, then.

                              JACK
Yeah.

                              BARRY
Yeah.

                              PATRICK
Thanks, Jack.

PATRICK gives JACK a big hug.

> JACK
>
> Any time, man.

> PATRICK
>
> I'll get you that cash back as soon as . . . as soon as I can.

> JACK
>
> Whenever.

PATRICK turns to BARRY, looking for a hug.

> BARRY
>
> A handshake will do for me, fruitcake.

> PATRICK
>
> Not for me, Barry.

PATRICK reaches out for him and BARRY begrugingly reciprocates. He then pushes PATRICK away.

> BARRY
>
> That's enough.

◘INT: JACK AND MOLLY'S BEDROOM. EVENING

JACK is looking out the bedroom window. MOLLY walks over to him and they embrace. Things are going to be all right.

◘INT: AUDREY'S APARTMENT. DAY

AUDREY is in her apartment, packing. The phone rings.

> AUDREY
>
> Hello? . . . No, Marty, Barry's not here right now. . . . Yeah, he should be here soon. Everything's fine. I—listen, I got to go. Can't talk right now. 'Bye.

■EXT: AUDREY'S STREET. SAME DAY

BARRY walks up AUDREY'S front stoop.

■INT: AUDREY'S APARTMENT. SAME DAY

BARRY enters AUDREY'S apartment. She is just finishing packing her bags.

> BARRY
>
> What's going on with all these bags?

> AUDREY
>
> All your stuff's in the blue bag.

> BARRY
>
> What do you mean? You going someplace?

> AUDREY
>
> I'm moving out.

> BARRY
>
> What do you mean? Where are you going?

> AUDREY
>
> I'm going home to New Jersey to take care of my dad for a while.

> BARRY
>
> How come?

> AUDREY
>
> What do you mean, how come? 'Cause you're a coward.

> BARRY
>
> Hey, I just don't think this is the right time for me to get involved in a serious relationship.

AUDREY

And why is that? Because as a big-time director you can't be tied down? Don't want to miss out on all the action you could be getting?

BARRY

What is that? Is that what you think? Is that why you think I'm breaking this off?

AUDREY

Can you give me another reason?

BARRY

Yeah, because I'm going to be busy. You know? I mean, I'm not going to have time for this. For us.

AUDREY

You know what? You can have this back, I don't want it.

AUDREY pulls the Claddah ring off and shoves it into his chest.

BARRY

Hey, Audrey, you knew from day one that I wasn't interested in letting this become, you know, too serious.

AUDREY

I don't care what we thought was going to happen. I fell in love with you, and I think you fell in love with me too. Didn't you?

BARRY

Come on. You know, let's not get into this, all right?

AUDREY

Just answer the question, it won't kill you.

BARRY

What do you want me to say? All right . . . I mean . . . okay, yeah, I do love you.

AUDREY

Then why are you doing this?

BARRY

Because, you know what? I don't want to be in love. All right,
and I don't want a wife and I don't want a family either.

AUDREY

Whoever said anything about marriage and a family?

BARRY

I'm sorry, Audrey, it just can't be.

*Silence. They stand there looking at each other, neither one sure what to do or say
next. The phone rings.*

AUDREY

Go ahead and answer, it's Marty. You got what you wanted.

BARRY goes for the phone, and AUDREY goes for the door.

BARRY

Hello?

AUDREY picks up her bags and is almost out the door.

BARRY

Hey, Marty, hold on a second. . . . Hey, Audrey, wait a second.
I'm sorry it had to be like this.

AUDREY

I love you, Barry. And I'll never love anyone the way I love you.
But I'm not going to be like your mama and wait thirty-five
years for you.

AUDREY turns and exits.

BARRY

Hey, Audrey, come on, hold up.

BARRY looks down at the ring in his hand.

BARRY

Hey, Marty, sorry about that. . . . No, no, it's nothing. . . . Yeah,
you know what? Listen, I . . . I can't . . . I can't talk about
this. . . . All right, I got to go. I got to go.

BARRY hangs up the phone and runs off to look for her.

◼EXT: AUDREY'S STREET. SAME DAY

BARRY takes off down the street. As he gets to the corner, he sees what he thinks is AUDREY in a cab pulling away. BARRY is crushed. Just then AUDREY appears behind him.

AUDREY

Hey, Barry.

BARRY spins around. They both smile. AUDREY drops her bags and they kiss.

Fade to black.

She's the One

Fade in:

◻INT: FITZPATRICK HOUSE/KITCHEN. EARLY MORNING

A close-up of ice cubes covering the bottom of a large portable cooler. Suddenly, a case of Bud cans is thrown into the cooler, immediately followed by three peanut butter and jelly sandwiches in small Ziploc bags. The cooler is closed.

◻EXT: FITZPATRICK HOUSE/BACKYARD/DOCK. EARLY MORNING

The sun has just risen. With a cigar stub in his mouth, MR. FITZPATRICK, a lean silver-haired man of sixty, steps out of his small two-story Brooklyn home and across his back porch, carrying the cooler. A retired NYC fireman, he rarely goes anywhere without an FDNY baseball hat or one of various FDNY sweatshirts and T-shirts. Today is no exception.

FITZPATRICK'S backyard sits on a small channel where most of the homeowners have their own docks and boats. FITZPATRICK carries the cooler down the wooden stairs that lead to his dock and throws the cooler in the back of his boat, a fine twenty-eight-footer.

■INT: FITZPATRICK HOUSE/KITCHEN. MORNING

MICKEY FITZPATRICK, a young working-class guy, sits at the kitchen table reading the paper and drinking coffee. He is barely awake. MR. FITZPATRICK enters from outside and slaps his son on the back.

> MR. FITZPATRICK
> Cigar?

> MICKEY
> No. No, I'm going to wait till we get out there.

> MR. FITZPATRICK
> You about ready to go?

> MICKEY
> Yeah. Yeah, I'm ready.

> MR. FITZPATRICK
> Where's your sister?

> MICKEY
> He's in the bathroom primping himself. He thinks we're going to a fashion show, I guess.

MR. FITZPATRICK walks over to the bathroom door and kicks it open with his foot. The bathroom is offscreen.

> MR. FITZPATRICK
> Come on, sweetheart. While we're still young.

FRANCIS FITZPATRICK, called FRAN—a hotshot young Wall Streeter— steps out of the bathroom, his hair slicked back and polo shirt tucked and pressed.

> FRANCIS
> What do you think, Dad? You ever seen such a good-looking head of hair?

> MR. FITZPATRICK
> Just get your ass moving, pretty boy.

FRANCIS *grabs a cigar out of his father's shirt pocket and sticks it in his mouth.* FITZPATRICK *shakes his head and exits down the hallway.* FRANCIS *walks over to the table, sits down next to* MICKEY, *and lights his cigar.*

> FRANCIS
> Hey, tough guy. Don't want to start the first fishing trip of the summer off with a cigar, huh?

> MICKEY
> And you wonder why your breath stinks and your teeth are green, right?

> FRANCIS
> My teeth are not green, my man.

> MICKEY
> Yeah, but they sure as shit ain't white either.

MR. FITZPATRICK *reappears in the hallway. He's ready to get out there.*

> MR. FITZPATRICK
> Come on, ladies, I'm not gonna have you start the summer off with your bickering. Come on, Mickey, let's go. And Francis, your brother's right. Go brush your teeth, will ya? Your breath's disgusting.

> MICKEY
> What did I tell you, my man?

MICKEY *gets up from the table and follows* MR. FITZPATRICK *out the back door.* FRANCIS *sits alone at the table and breathes into his hand, trying to smell his own breath. He winces at the truth.*

◻EXT: FITZPATRICK HOUSE/DOCK/CHANNEL. MORNING

In a close-up, we see that the name of the boat, The Fighting Fitzpatricks, *is painted in green on the back. As the boat pulls away from the dock, we reveal the three men, on board, heading out to sea. It's a beautiful summer morning.*

◘EXT: FITZPATRICK BOAT/SEA/CHANNEL. LATER

The Fighting Fitzpatricks is anchored in the middle of the channel under the Marine Parkway Bridge. With their lines in the water, the three men sit, talk, drink beer, and smoke cigars. MR. FITZPATRICK sits opposite his two boys and talks to them like schoolchildren.

> MR. FITZPATRICK
>
> I'm concerned for you, Mick. I think maybe it's time for you to get focused on something. You know, maybe get a job.

> MICKEY
>
> Dad, I've got a job.

> MR. FITZPATRICK
>
> That ain't a job, that's an excuse to avoid reality. You know, it's time you thought about settling down, sinking your teeth into something. Something that will give your life some meaning. Now, I'm not saying you've got to work on Wall Street with this one, but what about the fire department or a cop, something with some benefits?

> FRANCIS
> *(interrupting)*
>
> The way I see it is this. Ever since the "hairy ass incident," it's like you've been out of the game, running away from life instead of running towards it. I think it's a good time right now to turn around and start running towards life again. You know what I'm talking about?

> MICKEY
>
> Can I toss this asshole overboard? Is that all right?

> FRANCIS
>
> Hey, don't get that way with me, Mick. I'm just trying to help.

> MR. FITZPATRICK
>
> Shut up, Francis. But your sister's right. You need something with some stability.

> MICKEY
>
> You know, Dad, I don't need any stability. Because I'm happy right where I am.

FRANCIS

Big deal, you're happy. You're never gonna make any real money.

MICKEY

Who gives a shit? I mean, look at you; you make a pile of dough and you're miserable.

FRANCIS

What's that got to do with anything? Hey, and I'm not miserable, okay? I'm dissatisfied. That's what makes me a success.

Listening to this, MR. FITZPATRICK can only shake his head. He'll try a different, softer approach.

MR. FITZPATRICK

Now, Mickey, there's something I've been meaning to tell you since you've been back. I think you did the right thing. The last thing you needed to do was get married, especially to that one. The one thing you got to remember is this is your life, not theirs. You got to do what makes you happy first. Okay?

MICKEY just hangs his head.

K. C. BAILEY

◼EXT: GREENWICH VILLAGE STREET. DAY

A yellow cab starts to pull over to pick up a Wall Street suit on his way to work. Offscreen, we hear a loud whistle and the cab quickly crosses the street to reveal the source of the whistle, a sexy young girl carrying a suitcase. Her name is HOPE.

◼INT: CAB. DAY

HOPE, a very stylish and free-spirited woman in her early twenties, hops into the backseat of the cab.

> HOPE
>
> JFK, please.

We then reveal that the cabbie is MICKEY. He looks over his shoulder and smiles. HOPE smiles back. There's an immediate connection. The cab takes off.

◼INT: MICKEY'S CAB/LOWER MANHATTAN. DAY (CONT)

HOPE leans forward to talk to MICKEY.

> HOPE
>
> Hey, how are you doing?

> MICKEY
>
> I'm good. What about you? Where are you flying to?

> HOPE
>
> New Orleans.

> MICKEY
>
> Oh, yeah? Vacation or something?

> HOPE
>
> No. Actually, my best friend from high school is getting married. It's kind of a funny story.

MICKEY

Oh, yeah?

HOPE

Yeah. Her sink was clogged a few weeks ago so she called a plumber, and this really nice guy came over to fix it and she ended up having sex with him under the sink. So now she's gonna marry him.

MICKEY

This is your best friend, having sex under the sink?

HOPE

Uh-huh.

MICKEY

That's good to know.

HOPE

So, what about you? Are you married?

MICKEY

Me? No. I mean I was engaged once, a couple of years ago, but it didn't pan out.

HOPE

What happened?

MICKEY

Nothing, really. I just came home early one night to find her and some guy passed out on my living room floor. Both of them completely naked.

HOPE

Oh my God. Did you know the guy?

MICKEY

No, all I saw was his hairy ass staring back at me. But I think he may have been a plumber too, actually.

HOPE
(laughing)
What did you do?

MICKEY
Nothing, really. I walked out of the apartment, got into my car, and spent the next three years driving around the country.

HOPE
Wow. Do you have any regrets about it?

MICKEY
Yeah, yeah. One. I should have taken my friggin' TV with me when I left.

HOPE smiles and leans back in her seat.

◼EXT: JFK TERMINAL. SAME DAY

A crowded airport terminal. MICKEY carries HOPE'S bags from his cab toward the gate. She walks with him, a sly smile on her face.

HOPE
How long would it take me to drive to New Orleans?

MICKEY
Not that long. It's like, twenty-three, twenty-four hours, maybe.

HOPE
And how much would that cost?

MICKEY
I don't know. You could probably get a pretty cheap rental car here at the airport.

HOPE
Well, what if you drove me? How much would that be?

MICKEY

What do you mean? If I drove you in my cab? If I kept the meter running, it would cost you—I don't know—like seventy or eighty thousand dollars, maybe.

HOPE
(laughing)
Look, you could come to my friend's wedding. I'm allowed to bring a date.

MICKEY

You're serious about this? You want me to drive you to New Orleans in my cab?

HOPE

Yeah. Come on, please? It'll be fun. I really don't want to fly. And if I did and I died, then it would be all your fault. And I don't think you want to live with that guilt.

HOPE turns on her heels and heads back toward the cab. MICKEY quickly follows. He knows he's been beat.

MICKEY

My fault? You tell me why you're so afraid to fly, and then maybe I'll consider it.

HOPE

I don't like planes.

◘INT: FRANCIS'S LOFT. NIGHT

FRANCIS sits in bed working on his laptop. It's obvious from his apartment that he does all right on Wall Street. His wife, RENEE, returns home from a late night at the office and then appears at the bedroom door.

RENEE

Hey, babe.

FRANCIS

Hey.

RENEE enters and sits down next to FRANCIS. She rubs his leg.

RENEE

Busy?

FRANCIS

A little busy.

RENEE

Too busy to . . . I don't know, do it tonight?

FRANCIS

Do what, babe?

RENEE

Oh, I don't know, Francis. Why don't I take off my clothes and you can do whatever you'd like.

FRANCIS

Renee, come on. You know I've got to get this work done. How about a little consideration?

RENEE

How about a little consideration for me? You know we haven't had sex for a while, you know?

FRANCIS

All right, listen. . . . Okay. If you're still up when I have this finished, we'll do it, okay?

RENEE can't believe her ears. She jumps up from the bed.

RENEE

You know, don't do me any favors, all right there, Romeo? I can just as easily go into the bathroom and use my vibrator.

RENEE goes over to her closet and starts to change out of her work clothes.

FRANCIS

That would be a little difficult, wouldn't it? Seeing as you don't own a vibrator?

RENEE

Babe, what's the big deal with me owning a vibrator?

FRANCIS

No big deal. You just don't have one.

RENEE

Okay.
(heads back over to the bed)
Occasionally, I need sex, and for some reason I'm married to a man who doesn't like to have sex anymore, so from time to time I like to pleasure myself with a vibrator. Deal with it.

RENEE spins out of the bedroom. FRANCIS quickly follows her to the door.

FRANCIS

Excuse me? Pleasure yourself? That's rich. And no, I'm not going to deal with it. Because you're my wife. We have sex like normal people, in a bed, lying down. We don't run to bathrooms and masturbate like animals with any friggin' vibrators.

RENEE returns in the bedroom with a basket of laundry, which she throws on the bed.

RENEE

Okay. Maybe you don't, but I do. So unless you wake up that libido of yours, I'm in that bathroom in about five minutes. Better yet, I could go get it and we could play with it together.

Offscreen, we hear a man's whistle from the street below.

FRANCIS

Okay. Very funny. Listen, let's get this straight once and for all, funny girl. We do not have a vibrator in this home. Do we?

Again offscreen, we hear the whistle and a MAN calling what sounds like "Francis!" RENEE smiles.

RENEE

Better go see who that is.

RENEE smiles and exits the room. FRANCIS goes to the window and looks down to the street.

◘EXT: FRANCIS'S APT. BUILDING/STREET. NIGHT (CONT)

MICKEY is standing outside by his cab, with HOPE sitting on the hood right next to him.

> MICKEY
> Hey, Franny. It's me, Mickey.

FRANCIS opens the window.

> FRANCIS
> Yeah, I can see that. What the hell are you doing?

> MICKEY
> Hey, man, you're not gonna believe this. I got married. Why don't you let us up? I want you to meet my wife.

RENEE runs to the window and sticks her head out.

> RENEE
> Hey, Mickey. Congratulations. When did this happen?

> MICKEY
> Let us up and I'll tell you all about it.

> FRANCIS
> Yeah. Hold on a second, babe.

◘INT: FRANCIS'S LOFT. NIGHT (CONT)

FRANCIS pulls his head back into the apartment and turns to RENEE.

> FRANCIS
> He wants to come up.

> RENEE
> Yeah, I heard. What's your problem? I would like to meet her.

FRANCIS
Hon, it's late, you're not thinking straight.

FRANCIS sticks his head back out the window.

FRANCIS
Hey, Mick, we're glad you're living such a romantic life, the both of us. But hey, some people have some real jobs—you know, responsibilities. Catch you tomorrow; give me a call. Congratulations, though.

MICKEY
Hey, fuck you, you prick. Come down and let us in.

FRANCIS
I'm going to let you into my home in the middle of the night after you don't invite me to your wedding?

RENEE
(sticking her head out)
Mickey, don't listen to him. Of course you can come up. I'm going to send him down right now.

RENEE and FRANCIS pull their heads back in and close the window.

FRANCIS
Excuse me? What are you talking about? I'm going to let this man into our home in the middle of the night after he doesn't invite me to his wedding?

RENEE
Oh, you are sick.

FRANCIS
Oh, I'm sick. I'm not the one with the vibrator. You know, if I find that thing I'm going to mail it to your mother with a nice detailed letter describing your perversions.

RENEE
Go right ahead. Who do you think got me the damn thing in the first place? Okay. She knows my pain.

◻INT: FRANCIS'S LOFT/KITCHEN. NIGHT (CONT)

FRANCIS and RENEE'S apartment is a large beautiful Soho loft. RENEE, FRANCIS, MICKEY, and HOPE sit around the kitchen table, drinking coffee and smoking cigarettes.

> HOPE
>
> Anyway, we were having a great time together on the drive down, and I guess it was sometime after we crossed into Kentucky that we fell in love. And then Mickey came with me to my friend's wedding and when we were dancing he said it should have been us who got married. So I ran over and got the priest out of the bar and dragged him onto the dance floor, and he married us right there in the middle of the reception.

> RENEE
>
> Ohhh. I want to get married like that. Mickey, do you have any other brothers I don't know about?

> MICKEY
>
> Sorry, babe, just princess kitty over there. I think you're stuck with him.

RENEE

That's it, huh?

FRANCIS

Is this true, Mick?

MICKEY

What can I say, man? I'm all about the love.

FRANCIS

Obviously! I had no idea you were such an impetuous romantic.
I mean, that's a pretty impulsive move you guys pulled. But I'm
sorry, when did you guys actually meet?

HOPE

Wednesday.

FRANCIS

Oh, and today is Saturday. Okay. So you were married without a
best man on when?

HOPE

Thursday.

FRANCIS

Oh, so you had a full twenty-four hours to get to know each
another.

RENEE

Oh, Francis!

FRANCIS

No, I'm relieved, honey. Aren't you? I mean, I thought they
might have rushed into this.

MICKEY

Watch yourself, Francis.

RENEE

You know what, guys? Don't listen to Francis. He's about as
impulsive and romantic as a nun. In fact, you know what,

honey? I'm wondering why you actually didn't become one.

FRANCIS shoots her a look and places his hand on RENEE'S arm.

FRANCIS
So am I, honey.

HOPE
(cutting them off)
You probably don't know your brother as well as you think you do. He's actually very romantic.

HOPE leans over and kisses MICKEY on the cheek.

MICKEY
I don't think we need to go there right now, thank you.

FRANCIS
No, let's go there by all means. Mr. Romantic. Mr. Summer Breeze, "all about the love." Of course, you're right. What would I know? I'm just the brother who wasn't the best man.

FRANCIS gets up and starts to leave the kitchen.

RENEE
Oh, Francis, you're going to have to get over this.

FRANCIS
Nothing to get over, hon. I'm thrilled, couldn't be more. Congratulations, guys. Romance is wonderful; we all love it; it brightens the day. I just want to remind you, it don't pay the rent.

FRANCIS exits. HOPE looks to MICKEY, who can offer no explanation. She tries RENEE.

HOPE
Is he okay?

RENEE
Yeah, he'll live.

◘ EXT: HOPE'S BUILDING. NIGHT

MICKEY and HOPE walk down a cobblestone West Village street carrying boxes and a suitcase. They come to Hope's place, a run-down tenement.

> HOPE
> This is it.

> MICKEY
> This is the honeymoon suite, huh?

MICKEY hesitantly follows HOPE up the front stoop.

◘ INT: HOPE'S BUILDING/HALLWAY. NIGHT (CONT)

MICKEY comes laboring up the stairs. HOPE turns and drops the bag on top of one of the boxes he is carrying. She then opens the door for him and MICKEY enters the apartment. She waits out in the hall. MICKEY then reappears, picks her up in his arms, and carries her over the threshold.

◘ EXT: FITZPATRICK HOUSE/BACKYARD. DAY

MR. FITZPATRICK is in the backyard cooking steaks at the barbecue. FRANCIS watches and lights a cigarette.

> MR. FITZPATRICK
> What do you think's going on? What is she, an illegal? Pregnant? What?

> FRANCIS
> Maybe an illegal. She looks like she's from one of the islands.

> MR. FITZPATRICK
> Yeah, I was thinking the same thing. You know, I'm concerned for him, Francis. Do you think it will last?

> FRANCIS
> No shit! Are you kidding me?

MR. FITZPATRICK

Poor kid. Never used up here.
(points to his head)
Always used in here.
(points to his heart).
Just like your mother.

FRANCIS
(getting teary-eyed)
I just can't believe he did it without me. Frankly, I should have
been there. I should have been his best man. He was my best
man. And just for the record, it's bad luck to have a wedding
without a best man.

MR. FITZPATRICK

Oh, Jesus, you're not crying, are you, Francis?

◼ INT: FRANCIS'S OFFICE. DAY

*FRANCIS, dressed in an expensive suit, stands behind his desk, talking on the
phone and admiring his view of lower Manhattan and the river.*

FRANCIS
(screaming)
No, no! I am not interested in what they have to say, I am
interested in you doing what you're told. Now, when you've
done that, call me back. No, have Ryan call me!

*FRANCIS slams down the phone and lights up another butt. His secretary
buzzes in.*

SECRETARY
(OS)
Mr. Fitzpatrick, I have Miss Davis on the phone.

FRANCIS
Yeah, yeah. Put her through. . . . Heather?

◼INT: PAPA'S APARTMENT/BEDROOM. SAME DAY

PAPA'S apartment has a sort of gaudy, lavish, old-world charm. HEATHER DAVIS, 24, a sexy blonde, lounges in bed, smoking a cigarette.

FRANCIS
Are you okay? I called the office this morning, and they said you called in sick today. I called the apartment and you're not there. Are you all right?

HEATHER
Yes, I'm fine. How's work?

FRANCIS
Work's fine. Where are you?

HEATHER
I'm at Papa's.

FRANCIS
Who the hell is Papa?

HEATHER
Come on, Franny, you know my friend Papa.

FRANCIS
Oh, you mean Carl, the old guy? Well, listen, I thought we agreed we were going to call him Carl the Diaper-Wearing Geriatric, not Papa! What the hell are you doing there?

HEATHER
I slept over here last night.
(pause)
With him.

FRANCIS
You mean you slept with him, as in: had actual sexual intercourse with this animal?

HEATHER
Among other things.

FRANCIS

That's not funny. He's older than your father, for God's sake.

HEATHER

Francis, my father's dead.

FRANCIS

My point exactly, thank you.
(pause)
This is very upsetting. I think it's extremely important that I see you as soon as possible so that I can show you the error of your ways here.

HEATHER

Well, he's going to be gone all day long, you know. You can come over to his place if you want.

FRANCIS

I'm afraid I still have my pride, darling. I'm not going to meet you at this old fucker's apartment. Okay?

HEATHER

Well, I guess you won't see me today, then, will you?

FRANCIS *thinks this over for a moment and then grabs a pen.*

FRANCIS

Okay, what's the address?

◻INT: PAPA'S BEDROOM. LATER THAT DAY

FRANCIS *leans back and lights up a cigarette, smiling.* HEATHER *then grabs his cigarette for herself.* FRANCIS *lights another.*

FRANCIS

Well, I hope that cleared things up for you.

HEATHER *smirks.*

FRANCIS

What? Excuse me! Don't even try to tell me sex with Grandpa was better than with me.

HEATHER

You're not in competition with him, Francis. Besides, one wasn't better than the other, they were just different.

FRANCIS

They better damn well be different. He's an old man who can't control his bladder and has to wear diapers, and I'm a young stallion in the prime of my youth.
(pause)
But how were we different?

HEATHER

It was just different. Forget I said anything.

FRANCIS

No, elaborate! I think it might be enlightening to understand how sex might be different with a fossil.

HEATHER

Don't get mad, all right?

FRANCIS nods confidently.

HEATHER

I faked my orgasm with you.

FRANCIS

So?

HEATHER

I didn't have to with Papa.

FRANCIS jumps out of bed and goes for his clothes.

FRANCIS

I got you.

HEATHER

Come on, Francis, don't be mad. You wanted to know.

FRANCIS

No, I really didn't.

HEATHER

Don't pull this jealous bullshit with me, okay? I can sleep with whomever I want. Remember, I'm not the one who's married, you are.

FRANCIS is taken aback. He thinks for a moment.

FRANCIS

You really had an orgasm with him?

HEATHER holds up three fingers.

◘INT: FRANCIS'S PRIVATE CAR. DAY

FRANCIS rides in the backseat of his private car. TOM, his driver, is a silver-haired gentleman with a hint of an Irish brogue.

FRANCIS

Pardon my asking, Tom, but how old are you?

TOM

Sixty-eight.

FRANCIS

You know I was just wondering, more out of curiosity than anything, if a guy your age can still have sex.

TOM .

Only when the wife gives me the okay.

FRANCIS

But you still can perform then, if she says so?

TOM

Sure. As a matter of fact, my wife says I'm better now than when I was in my twenties.

FRANCIS is crushed by this news. He slides back in his seat and sulks.

FRANCIS

Great. That's terrific, Tom.

◨EXT: STREET. DAY

Summer in the city. MICKEY walks HOPE down a cobblestone Village street on her way to work.

MICKEY
So this apartment of ours, how long have you lived there?

HOPE
Almost two years. Isn't it great?

MICKEY
Yeah, it is. It's a little small, though.

HOPE
But it's cozy.

MICKEY

Cozy? Yeah. You know, it's funny. When I took a shower this
morning there was no hot water, so that wasn't too cozy.

HOPE

Oh, yeah. I forgot to tell you. We never have hot water on the
weekends.

MICKEY

Really? Great! And there's a big hole in the ceiling of the
bathroom too. Because this morning it was funny; when I was
brushing my teeth, I had a nice view up some guy's boxer shorts.
That was real nice.

HOPE

That's Jim. You'll have to meet him; he's a good guy.

MICKEY

Oh, is he? Jim's a good guy? Good. I guess if I'm gonna be
looking at his pecker every morning, he may as well be a good
guy.

They stop in front of Tortilla Flats, a small Tex-Mex restaurant on the corner.

HOPE

I'd better get going. This is where I work.

MICKEY

Right here, huh? You know, it looks like it might get a little
chilly in there. And seeing as you're standing here practically
naked, I could run home and get you like a nice big down
jacket or a sweatsuit or something . . . because that might
help.

HOPE

I don't think so. I'll see you later. 'Bye.

HOPE leans in and gives MICKEY a kiss.

MICKEY

All right, take it easy.

HOPE

'Bye.

HOPE *enters the restaurant.*

□INT: TORTILLA FLATS. DAY (CONT)

The restaurant is empty except for CONNIE, who stands behind the bar cleaning glasses. Connie is HOPE'S sexy and quirky best friend.

HOPE

Hey, babe. What's up?

HOPE *grabs her apron off the bar and starts to get to work. CONNIE comes out from behind the bar and is hot on her heels.*

CONNIE

Was that him?

HOPE

Cute, huh?

CONNIE

I don't know. I thought he kind of looked like a real jerk.

HOPE

Thanks, Connie, that's really sweet of you.

CONNIE

No. I'm sorry. I know—I mean, he's probably a really nice guy. But did you have to marry him?

HOPE

Absolutely!

CONNIE

So I guess you're going to Paris with him instead of me, then?

HOPE

Well, we really haven't discussed that yet, but . . .

CONNIE

Oh, well, it's nice to see you're being up-front and honest with him at the start of this relationship. That's good.

HOPE

Hey! I've only known him a week. I haven't had a chance to tell him my life story yet, all right? Give me a break.

HOPE exits into the kitchen, leaving CONNIE talking to herself.

CONNIE

No, no. I understand. However, it will just be interesting to see how a cabdriver from Brooklyn feels about moving to Paris. That's all. He'll probably be fine with it. No big deal, he'll just move to Paris with you. . . .

◘EXT: BEACH CLUB. MORNING

RENEE'S family's cabana sits at the end of a long row of small beach cottages close to the ocean. Her family is a loud, loving, and very tan Long Island clan. Renee's mother, CAROL, her father, RON, her sister, MOLLY, and RENEE are sitting at the picnic table having lunch. FRANCIS flicks a cigarette into the sand and joins them.

FRANCIS

It will never last. Believe me, it will be a nightmare when they get to know each other.

RON

Maybe they were made for each other. Those things can happen, you know. Carol and I met right here at the beach club in 1963 by the pool on a Friday morning. By Saturday night, I had her in the dunes.

CAROL

Jesus, Ron! They don't need to hear all the details.

RON

We've been together ever since. There's something to be said for that.

MOLLY

All right, all right. Enough about the dunes! So what's going on, Franny? How are things down on Wall Street?

FRANCIS

Things are good.

RON

Things are good? You're a twenty-five-year-old kid and you make half a million a year. I would say things are better than good.

FRANCIS

I hate to spoil the illusion, Ron, but I don't make that kind of money.

RON

Hey, Francis, don't bullshit a bullshitter, okay? And by the way, it's been awhile since you gave your favorite father-in-law a nice inside tip.

MOLLY

Yeah, and what about setting me up with some of your rich friends?

RENEE

Excuse me, but my husband has some ethics. He is not some sort
of cheating sleezebag.

RON

You don't want to share the wealth anymore, huh, kid?

CAROL
(whispering to Ron)
It's not the only thing he don't want to share anymore.

RENEE overhears this while FRANCIS is oblivious.

RENEE

Mom, would you please!

CAROL

What, are you getting greedy in your old age, Fran?

RENEE

You know, it's really nice to come out here and see you guys
on the weekends. I mean, it's a wonder we don't do it more
often.

RON

Hey! Don't go and get sarcastic with us, young lady. We're your
parents, and therefore you are in no position to approve or
disapprove of what we say or do. Understand?

CAROL

Your father's right, right, right!

RENEE

Really? Well, my analyst is going to have a field day with that bit
of psychosis. If you two lunatics will excuse me, I'm going to go
play some tennis.

RENEE gets up from the table and walks away.

RON

Her analyst?

CAROL

Don't ask.

*RON shrugs and pops his cigar into his mouth. FRANCIS leans over and
whispers to RON as he lights his father-in-law's cigar.*

FRANCIS

MacroCom. I'll call you on Monday.

◘ INT: HOPE'S APARTMENT. EARLY MORNING

*A seedy but quaint Greenwich Village studio apartment: high ceilings, pink walls,
and creaky floors. MICKEY exits the bathroom, putting on his watch, and walks
over to the mantel. He picks up a framed photograph of HOPE and
CONNIE.*

*He then looks over to HOPE, who is asleep in their pull-out convertible
bed/couch. MICKEY then walks over to HOPE and kneels down beside her.
She opens her eyes.*

MICKEY

Hey, babe. I'm going to go to work now.

HOPE

Okay. Love me?

MICKEY

Yeah, of course I do.

HOPE

Good. 'Cause I love you. 'Bye.

MICKEY

'Bye.

MICKEY leans over and kisses HOPE.

◻EXT: STREET. DAY

MICKEY'S CAB pulls over to drop off a fare.

◻INT: MICKEY'S CAB. DAY

The gentleman in the cab pays MICKEY and slips out the door. A young woman then jumps into his place. She slips off her sunglasses. It's HEATHER. Looking great. And out of his league.

HEATHER

Seventy-fifth and Madison, please.

MICKEY starts to take off and looks in the rearview mirror. He recognizes her. HEATHER is busy looking through her purse. They drive through Central Park.

MICKEY

So, Seventy-fifth and Madison, huh? That's a pretty swanky address.

HEATHER
(annoyed)

Excuse me?
(looking up)

Oh, my God. Mickey?

MICKEY

Yep.

HEATHER

What are you doing?

MICKEY

I'm in shock is what I'm doing. What are you doing?

They are both nervous and uncomfortable.

HEATHER

I'm . . . I'm going home. What about you? How have you been?

MICKEY

I've been good.

HEATHER

Good. Everything's all right?

MICKEY

Yeah. Everything's fine. What about you? You look like you must finally be making some decent money.

HEATHER

Well, you know, still on Wall Street. Not making as much money as I'd like. . . .

MICKEY

Yeah, well, you were never easy to please, right? So, are you married yet?

HEATHER

No, he hasn't asked just yet.

MICKEY

Oh, really? Not that hairy ape who was sprawled out on my carpet, I hope.

HEATHER

No. Not him.

MICK

Well, I can't say I blame you. I mean, what I did see of him wasn't too pretty. A little on the furry side. So who is this prospective husband? Anybody I know?

HEATHER

No, I don't think so. He and his friends have real jobs.

MICKEY takes the jab and smiles.

MICKEY

Yeah, right. You know, from anyone else I would take that as an insult. But you seem to forget the fact that I know how you put yourself through college.

HEATHER

Somebody had to pay for my education, sweetheart.

AN UNCOMFORTABLE SILENCE.

HEATHER

You had to bring that up, right?

MICKEY

An eye for an eye.

◻INT: HEATHER'S APARTMENT. DAY

HEATHER *steps into the room, removing her suit jacket.*

HEATHER

Okay. I've made up my mind. I can't go through with this.
If you're going to take the TV, I think it's only fair that you
give me back the watch. I mean, it *is* the watch I gave you,
right?

MICKEY *appears opposite her, carrying his old TV. He looks ridiculous.*

MICKEY

Yeah, it is. But like you said, the watch was a gift. And the TV
wasn't.

HEATHER
(smiling)
But if I recall correctly, I did pay for part of that TV. I mean, it's
not like you could afford it on your own.

MICKEY *laughs. He puts the TV down and takes off the watch.*

MICKEY

Okay. You want the watch, you can have the watch. It doesn't
really mean that much to me anyhow.

HEATHER
(grabbing his hand)
It's not the watch I want, Mickey.

MICKEY *pulls away, hands her the watch, and grabs his TV.*

MICKEY

Yeah, why don't we just give that a break already, okay,
Heather?

HEATHER

Give you a break? You mean to tell me that you actually came up here for the TV?

MICKEY

Yeah. Why do you think I came up here?

HEATHER

You're so full of shit.

MICKEY

Oh, yeah? And how do you figure that?

HEATHER

You can honestly say that you don't even think of me anymore?

MICKEY

Yeah, sure, of course I think about you. I think, What could have possibly possessed you to take that dirtbag home to my apartment?

MICKEY exits past her and up the spiral staircase, still carrying the television. HEATHER follows.

HEATHER

Come on, Mickey. We both knew the relationship was over before that. I wanted a career and you wanted . . . who the hell knows what you wanted? Did you ever figure that out?

MICKEY

Yeah, you know what? As a matter of fact, I did.

MICKEY steps into the living room. HEATHER walks right past him and sits down on her couch. MICKEY follows and stands above her. The TV is getting heavier.

HEATHER

Oh, that's right. Your brother told me you got married.

MICKEY

What do you mean, my brother? Since when do you speak to Francis?

HEATHER hesitates and then smiles.

HEATHER

Well, you know, he and his friends have real jobs, so occasionally
I run into him.

MICKEY finally takes a seat opposite her, resting the television on his knees.

MICKEY

You know, it's a shame he's married. You two probably would
have hit it off.

HEATHER

Maybe.
                                    (pause)
Anyhow, I'm just sorry you had to find out the way you did. I
would have liked to have been friends.

MICKEY

Friends? Really? You know what, Heather? I don't think that
would have worked, actually, because I have this thing and I try
to keep the number of friends who lie and cheat me to a
minimum.

HEATHER

Oh, please, Mickey. Put your fucking sanctimonious bullshit to
rest already.

MICKEY

I'm sorry. I guess the fact that I've always tried to behave like a
decent human being has rubbed you the wrong way, hasn't it?

HEATHER

Well, look where your decency has gotten you. You're the only
English-speaking white guy driving a cab in New York. That
should tell you something.

MICKEY looks long and hard at her. He stands up and heads to the door.

MICKEY

You know what, Heather? I've got to imagine it beats sucking
dick for a living, though, huh?

HEATHER

Depends on whose dick it is.

MICKEY just shakes his head as he walks out the door.

◼ INT: HOPE'S BUILDING/STAIRWELL. SAME DAY

MICKEY, TV in his arms, struggles up two flights of stairs toward his apartment. JIM, from upstairs, passes Mick on his way down.

MICKEY

Hey, Jim.

JIM

Hey, Mick.

MICKEY

How they hangin', man?

JIM

Hanging fine, thanks.

◼ INT: HOPE'S APARTMENT. SAME DAY

A sticky New York summer afternoon. MICKEY lugs the television over to the kitchen table. HOPE sits at her desk doing schoolwork.

MICKEY

Hey, babe.

HOPE

Hey.

MICKEY

It's friggin' hot in here. What happened?

MICK goes over to give HOPE a kiss hello.

HOPE

Yeah, I know. We lost our electricity again.

MICK

Oh, really? Great! You know, I really love this place.

HOPE

Oh, just grab a beer if you want to cool off.

MICKEY disappears into the kitchen.

MICKEY

Well, you know, Hope, I don't mean to point out the obvious, but usually the fridge doesn't work if there's no electricity.

MICKEY reappears with his beer.

HOPE

How is it?

MICKEY

It's good, it's really good. It's got a nice warm-piss quality to it, you know?

HOPE

Oh, you're in a good mood, huh?
                    (taking notice of the TV)
So what's with the TV?

MICKEY

Oh, you like it? I figured we needed a TV.

HOPE

Yeah. No, it's fine, but where'd you get it?

MICKEY

It's funny you should ask.
            (heads away from Hope's glare)
I picked up . . . um . . . Heather in my cab today, and I told you she had the TV, so, you know, I basically told her I wanted my TV back.

HOPE

Oh, really? And then what happened?

MICKEY

Well, I went to her apartment, I got the TV, and I carried it
out.

HOPE

You were up in your ex-fiancée's apartment today? And how
was that? Was it fun?

MICKEY

What are you doing? I went up there for the TV, that's it. What?
Are you mad at me?

HOPE

No.

*HOPE quickly turns and heads into the kitchen. MICKEY takes off after her
and wraps his arms around her.*

MICKEY

Hey, come on, Hope, all right. If there's one thing you don't
have to worry about, it's that, all right?

HOPE turns around in his arms.

HOPE

Yeah, I know. I'm allowed to get a little jealous sometimes, aren't
I?

MICKEY

No. Remember, I'm a good guy.

HOPE

Yeah, right. I've heard that song and dance before.
                    (heading back out of the kitchen)
So, does she have a nicer apartment than us?

MICKEY

Well, she has electricity, so that's kind of nice.

◼ EXT: SOHO STREET. DAY

RENEE and FRANCIS walk down the street carrying their dry cleaning and groceries. The following six scenes will be crosscut.

> RENEE
>
> I'm jealous of them.

> FRANCIS
>
> Don't be, please. Listen, he's a cabdriver; she's a waitress; they live in a fourth-floor walk-up with no electricity, okay?

> RENEE
>
> Yeah, but you see how they are always all over one another? I bet you they have sex all the time. Does he ever tell you stuff like that?

> FRANCIS
>
> What? Granted, this man is my brother, but I do not ask him how often he has sex with this girl.

◘INT: McHALE'S BAR. EVENING

FRANCIS and MICKEY are sitting at the bar having a few pints.

> **FRANCIS**
> What kind of numbers are we talking, five, six, seven times a day?

> **MICKEY**
> Listen, I'm not telling you anything. Okay?

◘EXT: SOHO STREET. DAY (CONT)

FRANCIS and RENEE walk on. Their conversation is picked up where we left them.

> **RENEE**
> I bet it's a lot. Remember how much we used to do it when we first got married?

> **FRANCIS**
> Yeah, sure. But honey, everybody's like that when they first meet. But then you get into a groove and you slow down. It would be impossible to keep up that level of intensity for an extended period of time. I mean, you'd hurt yourself.

◘INT: McHALE'S BAR. EVENING (CONT)

FRANCIS and MICKEY at the bar.

> **FRANCIS**
> That's why your back's all fucked up, huh? You've been doing it, what, round the clock, huh?

> **MICKEY**
> What kind of sick degenerate are you? Okay. This is my wife you're talking about.

◘EXT: SOHO STREET. DAY (CONT)

FRANCIS and RENEE walk. Again, we pick them up where they left off.

> RENEE
> I think we have a problem with our sex life.

> FRANCIS
> Listen, no, we don't. Unlike those two animals, we have real jobs and responsibilities. We don't have all day to rub up against each other. Our sex life is fine, believe me.

> RENEE
> Francis, I cannot remember the last time I saw your penis.

> FRANCIS
> What? Excuse me. What kind of language is that? We're on a public street here.

> RENEE
> Maybe we should get one of those sex improvement tapes, or I could get some stuff from Victoria's Secret. Maybe that would help.

> FRANCIS
> Honey, would you stop talking about this? Because it's depressing me. I told you. It's a down cycle, that's all.

◘INT: McHALE'S BAR. EVENING (CONT)

FRANCIS and MICK talk at the bar.

> FRANCIS
> What? You're not familiar with the down cycle?

> MICKEY
> No. What exactly is the down cycle?

FRANCIS

You know, in a relationship you've got ups, downs . . . sometimes
you do it a lot, like you do. Other times, not at all. Ups and
downs. The down cycle.

MICKEY

I feel for you, man. You're a sick individual, and you need help.

◨INT: SALVATION ARMY. DAY

*MICKEY and HOPE walk through rows and rows of used clothing in a
warehouse-sized Salvation Army.*

MICKEY

You know, Hope, I think maybe we should talk about our
apartment situation.

HOPE

Why? You don't like our apartment?

MICKEY

No, no, it's not that at all. I like the fact that we never have
electricity and hot water and I love the pink walls, you know
that. I'm just thinking it's maybe a little too small for two people?

HOPE

Yeah, I know. But there's a chance we'll only be there another
month, and then we might be moving to Paris.

MICKEY

Whoa, what do you mean, we might be moving to Paris? Why
would we ever move to Paris?

HOPE

Because I might be going to school there in the fall.

MICKEY

This is Paris, France, you're talking about?

HOPE

Yeah.

MICKEY
The country in Europe where they hate Americans?

HOPE
That's not true. They just don't like stupid Americans.

MICKEY
You know, Hope, unfortunately, I think I would probably fall
into that category. So when do you find out about this? I mean,
this is a fairly important development in our lives, don't you
think?

HOPE
I should find out if I got in this week.

MICKEY
(sarcastically)
Really? That's great. Thanks for letting me in on this. I really
appreciate it.

HOPE
You know, Mick, maybe your brother's right. This would be the
perfect time for you to run toward life.

◼INT: SOHO STORE. DAY

HEATHER *walks down an isle picking up skimpy lingerie and holding it up*
for Francis. FRANCIS is not amused.

HEATHER
Do you think this is something your little wife had in mind?

FRANCIS
Don't joke about that. She's still my wife.

HEATHER
(turning away from him)
All of a sudden he's got a conscience.

FRANCIS
Listen, I think it's time we started discussing our future.

HEATHER
What about this? Do you think she would like this?

She holds up another pair of underwear.

FRANCIS
Listen, I'm serious about this. We have to decide where this relationship is going.

HEATHER
Obviously, it's not going anywhere now, is it, Francis?

FRANCIS
No, obviously you don't understand. This relationship has to reach the next level, and we as a couple have to decide what that next level is.

HEATHER
Why the sudden urgency?

FRANCIS
Well, for one thing, I don't like the fact that you have sex with a geriatric.

HEATHER
Well, how do you think I feel about you going home and seeing your wife every night?

FRANCIS
I haven't had sex with my wife in months.

HEATHER
Well, I don't know if that's such a good idea, Francis. Clearly you need the practice.

◘EXT: FITZPATRICK HOUSE/PORCH. NIGHT

A quiet suburban summer night. FRANCIS and MR. FITZPATRICK are hanging on the back porch. FITZPATRICK has his cigar and pours himself an Irish whiskey.

MR. FITZPATRICK

You know, Francis, if you're afraid to ask her for a divorce, why don't you just have sex with her in the meantime?

FRANCIS

Dad, I'm in love with another woman. I don't think it would be fair to have sex with Renee.

MR. FITZPATRICK

Let me get this straight. You don't want to cheat on your girlfriend with your wife?

FRANCIS

Yeah. I guess so.

MR. FITZPATRICK

Jesus Christ, Francis. Are you sure I'm your father? You know, I'm going to have to double-check with your mother on this one.

FRANCIS

Come on, Dad. Be serious. How do you think Mom will take it?

MR. FITZPATRICK

She's gonna be devastated. She's been up at that goddamn church every morning praying for your brother. And then yesterday she tells me I spend too much time on the boat. I don't even want to get into that discussion. And now you're gonna get divorced? Christ. She'll be up with Father John twenty-four hours a day. Thanks a lot, buddy. I'm probably going to have to start making my own breakfast again.

FRANCIS

I'm sorry if my divorce interferes with your breakfast plans, Dad.

MR. FITZPATRICK

Hey. Don't get all sensitive on me now, Barbara. You know, all your life, you've always wanted to screw every good-looking skirt who walked by. And now that you're making all this money, you're probably finding that you can at least have half of them.

FRANCIS

Come on, Dad. What have you been telling me my whole life?
I've got to do what makes me happy first, right? Besides, that's
normal male behavior. We can't control millions of years of
evolution. You know what it's like? It's like you've been driving
a seventy-four Buick your whole life and suddenly you find
yourself behind the wheel of a brand-new Porsche. How do you
go back to the Buick?

MR. FITZPATRICK

Yeah, I guess you can't.

FRANCIS
(placing a hand on his dad's shoulder)
You know, Dad, I'm really doing this for Renee.

MR. FITZPATRICK

I'm sure she's going to be really thrilled.

MR. FITZPATRICK then gives FRANCIS a loving slap to the face and exits
past him.

◘ INT: MICKEY'S CAB. DAY

MICKEY and HOPE are in the front seat of his cab, driving an older couple in
the backseat. The cab pulls over and Mickey turns off the meter. The man steps
out and holds the door for his wife and she climbs out.

HOPE
(calling to the couple)
Happy anniversary!

MICKEY drives off. HOPE drapes her arm around his shoulder.

MICKEY

You really enjoyed that, didn't you?

HOPE

They were fun. Weren't they?

MICKEY

Yeah, they were a lot of fun, but they were also a twelve-dollar fare.

HOPE

Oh, they were sweet and it was their anniversary.

MICKEY

I'm very happy for them, but you know what? They looked like they could afford to pay twelve bucks. Whereas we, on the other hand, cannot.

HOPE

I'll pay the twelve dollars, Mr. Cheapo.

She crosses her arms and turns away from MICKEY.

MICKEY

Oh, really. And do you happen to have this twelve dollars on you, by any chance?

HOPE
(pouting)
No. Not right now. I'll give it to you later.

MICKEY

Great! You know, I don't mean to sound like a jerk, but next time you ask to come to work with me, remind me to say no.

HOPE

And all this time, I thought you were a romantic!

MICKEY

I am. But you know what it is? As long as it doesn't interfere with paying the rent on time.

HOPE

Mick, I would rather live in the back of this cab than let something like the rent get in the way of our romance. What do you have to say to that?

MICKEY

Okay. When you're right, you're right.
(thinks for a bit)
You know, speaking of backseats . . . I do know a little place
where we could park and maybe, you know, put this backseat
theory of yours to the test.

HOPE

Oh, yeah?

MICK

Yeah.

HOPE
(calling his bluff)
Let's go.

HOPE smiles.

◘EXT: EAST 56TH STREET. DAY

*The cab is parked at the end of the dead-end street, rocking up and down. The
Queensboro Bridge looms in the background. An OLDER WOMAN walks by
with her dog and stops to look in the rocking cab.*

OLDER WOMAN

Oh, my God!

The woman and dog scurry away.

◘INT: FRANCIS'S LOFT. DAY

Midafternoon. FRANCIS is on the phone. We catch him in mid-conversation.

FRANCIS

She's been out with her sister all day. Hold on. I think this is
her.

*FRANCIS looks over his shoulder as RENEE and her sister, MOLLY, enter
the loft after an afternoon of shopping. They head his way.*

FRANCIS

Listen, I'll call you later.

FRANCIS hangs up as the girls enter. RENEE gives him a kiss as MOLLY drops down into the couch and lights a cigarette.

RENEE

Hi, honey. Who was that?

FRANCIS

You know, what's-his-face, from work.

RENEE

Oh, you've been talking to him a lot lately.

FRANCIS sits down next to MOLLY. RENEE takes a seat opposite them and starts to open her mail.

MOLLY

Anyhow, your old friend Scott from college was talking to my friend Nicole—you know her; we went to camp with her sister Patty.

RENEE

Right, I know Nicole. She went to BU with Scott's brother David.

MOLLY

Well, anyhow, he was telling her that his divorce was just finalized.

RENEE
(sadly)

Oh!

FRANCIS
(suddenly interested)

Who got divorced?

RENEE

You know Scott Sherman.

MOLLY

Yeah, he caught his wife boning her dentist in the shower.

RENEE

Boning? That's charming.

FRANCIS

Oh! This is fatso, four-eyed, greasy-haired Scott? The computer geek tapping on the keyboard?

RENEE

He was not that fat.

FRANCIS

He was a three-hundred-pound sack of shit, hon. Maybe to you that's not fat. But what the hell, you loved the animal.

RENEE

Oh, that's really nice. And he was not three hundred pounds. He was slightly overweight, that's all. Right?

MOLLY

Renee, his tits were bigger than mine!

RENEE

All right. So he wasn't so skinny but he was a very smart, really sweet guy, which is a hell of a lot more than I can say for the two of you.

RENEE *stands and walks to the desk against the windows.*

FRANCIS

You better be sweet when you weigh five-o.

RENEE

What is your problem with Scott? He's just a shy, harmless guy. Do you have to be in competition with everybody?

FRANCIS

You know what, hon? If he's such a fucking sweetheart and I'm such a creep, why didn't you marry the fat pig?

RENEE

I don't know. If I'd known you were going to turn into such an asshole, maybe I would have.

FRANCIS is taken aback. MOLLY cuts in.

MOLLY

Well, fat or not, guess who's got his phone number?

RENEE

You? You have Scott's phone number? Well, you're not going to call him!

MOLLY

Of course I am. What do you think? You're the only one who's gonna marry rich? I need somebody to pick up my Bergdorf bills too, sweetheart.

RENEE

No! What . . . where are you from? You're my sister. There's supposed to be an honor code between siblings. You do not date your sister's ex-boyfriend.

FRANCIS

Hon, let her go out with him. What the fuck is the big deal, anyway? Unless you still have feelings for the yard ape?

RENEE

No, it has nothing to do with that, okay? This has to do with respect, that's all: respect. A word that the two of you are not very familiar with.

RENEE storms out of the room.

◘EXT: GRAMERCY PARK. DAY

HOPE and MICKEY round the corner, walking along the wrought-iron fence of the park. They are arm in arm.

HOPE

My friend Connie doesn't think we'll last another month.

MICKEY

Why would she say something like that?

HOPE

She thinks you're a jerk.

MICKEY

Why does she think I'm a jerk? I don't even know this person.

HOPE

Because you haven't said yes to Paris yet.

MICKEY

Yeah, well, you haven't been accepted yet either, have you?

HOPE

Well, I also told her about your brother and your father and those weird fishing trips you guys take.

MICKEY

Hey, don't go bashing the fishing trips, all right? That's a family tradition. Those trips are sacred.

HOPE

And you don't think it's weird that your mom never goes on the boat?

MICKEY

Listen, my dad has a rule. No women on the boat.

HOPE

You don't think that's a little strange, Mick?

MICKEY

I mean, yeah, it's strange. But that's the way my dad thinks, you know? He's from the old school.

HOPE

Okay. So what's Fran's excuse?

MICKEY

Well, Fran . . . Fran's got some issues.

HOPE

Yeah, I'd say so.

◘INT: HEATHER'S APARTMENT. DAY

HEATHER gets dressed after an afternoon romp. FRANCIS lies in the bed in his boxers putting a watch on. We recognize it as Mickey's old watch.

FRANCIS

What are you doing, getting me gifts? You didn't have to get me anything.

HEATHER

It was nothing. Do you like it?

FRANCIS

Yeah, of course, I love it. Hey, what happened to the TV?

HEATHER

What, your brother didn't tell you?

FRANCIS

My brother? Tell me what?

HEATHER

It was his TV. He came up here and got it.

FRANCIS

My brother, your ex-fiancé, was up in this apartment? When was this?

HEATHER

I don't know. A few weeks ago. He picked me up in his cab.

FRANCIS

You didn't want to share this with me?

HEATHER

Jesus, Franny! Since when do I have to tell you anything?

HEATHER heads down the mirrored hallway to the bathroom. FRANCIS jumps up out of bed to follow.

FRANCIS

Wait, wait, wait. So my brother came into your bedroom and took a TV? That's it?

HEATHER

(stopping at the bathroom door)

No, actually, I tried to get him in bed but he wasn't interested.

FRANCIS

That's very funny. You know he's married now? He picked up some psycho waitress and married her in his cab or some shit like that.

HEATHER

I know. You told me. Sort of surprising move coming from Mickey, don't you think? It would have been nice to see some of that impulsiveness when we were together.

FRANCIS

What the fuck does that mean?

HEATHER

Nothing.

HEATHER then closes the bathroom door in his face.

◘INT: HOPE'S APARTMENT. DAY

A knock on the door. MICKEY answers and FRANCIS, wearing a double-breasted suit, walks in.

MICKEY

Hey, Fran. What are you doing here?

FRANCIS
What? I can't come by to see my big brother?

MICKEY
Yeah, sure.

FRANCIS steps into the apartment and looks around as he lights a cigarette.

FRANCIS
Jesus Christ! What a fucking dump! Hey, I like the pink walls, though. Finally comfortable with that part of yourself, huh?

MICKEY
You can't just come in, sit down, and keep your mouth shut, right, moneybags? I mean that would just be too difficult for you, huh?

FRANCIS
Oh, sorry. I forgot Mr. Summer Breeze is so *sensitivo.* Hey, I like the TV, though. How did you swing that one, man? I thought you said you two were broke.

MICKEY
Yeah, we still are. But you actually won't believe this. I picked Heather up in my cab last week and we got to talking, and she said she still had my old TV. So I went up to her place and I took it. It was kind of strange seeing her again, you know?

FRANCIS
So you went back and took your TV?

MICKEY
Well, you see it sitting there, don't you?

FRANCIS
You didn't feel like a loser?

MICKEY
Why would I feel like a loser?

FRANCIS

Oh, I don't know. Three years go by and you scurry back for a
TV? It's like admitting you're a failure and you can't afford a
new TV.

MICKEY

How the hell do we have the same blood pumping through our
veins? Do you really think I give a shit what Heather thinks
about me? I mean, come on, Franny.

FRANCIS

So, did you fuck her?

MICKEY

Did I what?

FRANCIS

When you were up at the apartment? Did you put it to her? Did
you bang her?

MICKEY

What do you think, I'm some kind of degenerate? You think
I'm some sort of immoral skell who cheats on his wife? Listen, I
don't cheat on my wife, okay?

FRANCIS

Oh, so you didn't fuck her?

MICKEY

It just dawned on me, Franny. You haven't fully evolved yet, have
you?

FRANCIS

Mick, come on. I mean, you almost married this woman. Then
you're going to be alone in her apartment to get a TV? I don't
buy it.

MICKEY

What do you want to hear? Do you want to hear that I had sex
with her? I mean, would that make you happy? All right, yeah, I
did her. I did her on the kitchen table, we did it on the couch,

we even did it on the friggin' TV; it was beautiful. I mean, I think you would have been proud of me.

> FRANCIS
> Hey, play all the games you want to play, Mick, but I'm a man. I know what I know.

> MICKEY
> You know what you know. Listen, you know what, Franny? I don't need this shit from you, okay? I don't need you to come over to my apartment and bust my hump. Why don't you just do me a favor and get the hell out of here, okay?

> FRANCIS
> Sure. I'll do you that favor.

FRANCIS takes another drag from his cigarette and heads past MICKEY toward the door. He then stops before exiting and slouches against the wall.

> FRANCIS
> I'm sorry, Mick. I'm feeling so guilty about this fucking divorce. I shouldn't feel guilty about that, right?

> MICKEY
> No, you shouldn't. What you should feel guilty about, though, is fucking that other woman for the last six months. That's what you should feel guilty about.

MICKEY picks up his newspaper and turns his back on FRANCIS.

◘ INT: FRANCIS'S PRIVATE CAR. SAME DAY

FRANCIS and his driver, TOM, heading back to the office.

> FRANCIS
> Tom, if you were single, would you date your brother's ex-girlfriend?

> TOM
> I don't have a brother, Mr. Fitzpatrick.

FRANCIS

But if you did, is that off limits?

TOM

I would have to say that only the lowest of the low, a real
scumbag, would date his brother's ex. There is a code between
siblings.

FRANCIS

Thanks, Tom.

◻ INT: HOPE'S RESTAURANT. LATE NIGHT

*The Isley Brothers' "Who's That Lady" blasts over the stereo. MICKEY sits at
the corner bar and CONNIE, HOPE'S friend and bartender, brings him a beer
and a glass. She slams down the beer on the bar, which sprays some beer onto
MICKEY'S face.*

MICKEY
(sarcastically)

Thanks!

CONNIE smiles and then leans into MICKEY from across the bar.

CONNIE

She's beautiful, isn't she?

MICKEY

Yeah, she really is.

CONNIE

You know she got her acceptance letter today?

MICKEY

Yeah, I know. She showed it to me.

CONNIE

You better go with her to Paris, all right? It's bad enough you
broke my heart when you swept her off her feet. I'm absolutely
not going to let any man hurt her again, okay?

MICKEY

Broke your heart? How did I manage to break your heart? I
mean, what did I just meet you five minutes ago?

CONNIE

My heart belongs to Hope. I love her.

MICKEY

You love her?

CONNIE

Yeah.

MICKEY

Do you guys have some sort of special relationship that maybe I
should be aware of, seeing as I'm married to her?

CONNIE

She didn't tell you?

MICKEY

No, she seems to have forgotten to mention it, actually.

CONNIE

Oh, no, nothing like that, nothing sexual or anything.

MICKEY

Good, that's a good thing.

CONNIE
(leaning in even farther)
But who knows, maybe if I'm lucky, one day you'll let me share
her with you?

*CONNIE smirks and walks away to the far end of the bar. MICKEY is
somewhat shocked as he waits for HOPE to come his way. He watches as
HOPE and CONNIE touch hands as they pass each other. HOPE smiles at
MICKEY as she walks down to his end of the bar.*

HOPE

Hey.

MICKEY

Yeah, your friend Connie here, she claims you guys have some sort of special relationship or something.

HOPE

Did she ask if you would share me?

MICKEY

Yeah, she asked about that.

HOPE

What do you think of that?

MICKEY
(stuttering and stumbling)
Well, you know, to be perfectly honest, the idea of two women at once seems like a very pleasant way to spend an evening. But, ah . . . not if one of the girls is my wife. And I'm not interested in doing it with anyone else. So, yeah . . . no.

HOPE

You better believe you don't want to do it with anyone else.

MICKEY

But you and her . . . ? I mean, you guys never actually consummated this love that she speaks of?

HOPE
(enjoying his discomfort)
No!

MICKEY

It does paint a pretty mental picture, though. And I hear it's very popular in Paris. The whole ménage-à-trois thing is French, isn't it?

HOPE

Don't get too smart, funny man. So are you going to come?

MICKEY

To Paris? I don't know. I mean, you're definitely gonna do this?

HOPE

Yes.

MICKEY

Yeah, well, I guess I gotta go, right?

HOPE

I guess so.

HOPE turns and goes back to work, leaving MICKEY alone at the bar.

◘EXT: BATTERY PARK. AFTERNOON

FRANCIS, in another expensive suit, walks along the water with MICKEY. People are out on their lunch breaks enjoying the sun.

FRANCIS

So, you're really gonna move to Paris?

MICKEY

Yeah, I guess it looks that way.

FRANCIS

Wow. Well, I bet you didn't count on that when you met her, huh?

MICKEY

I don't know, Fran. I'm starting to feel confused about this thing, you know?

FRANCIS

What, are you kidding me?

MICKEY

I don't know. It's like, I don't even know this girl. She's got these weird friends, she loves this dump we live in, and now all of a sudden she brings up this moving-to-Paris thing. And . . . you remember our little discussion about me going over to Heather's that day?

FRANCIS

Yeah?

MICKEY

I mean, I don't know. That's got me freaked out too, you know?
Part of me wanted to hate her and part of me wanted to . . . I
don't know. There was a weird connection there. You know? I
mean, we almost got married a few years ago.

FRANCIS

Mick, come clean. You fucked her.

MICK

Franny, don't start, all right?

FRANCIS

Mick, come on. You're talking about a weird connection here.
What, are you still in love with her?

MICKEY

No. It's nothing like that.

FRANCIS

Well, what? Did she say she was in love with you, or . . . ?

MICKEY

No, I'm just saying, it was weird seeing her again, that's all. But it
was nothing. Forget I said it.

FRANCIS nods, and they walk on in silence.

◘INT: HOPE'S APARTMENT. DAY

MICKEY is on the phone, mid-conversation.

MICKEY

Yeah, I can meet you there. . . . Forty-sixth and Eighth? All
right.

MICKEY hangs up the phone and thinks for a moment.

◼EXT: McHALE'S PUB. ESTABLISHING SHOT: DAY

◼INT: McHALE'S PUB. DAY

A quiet sunny afternoon in the Hell's Kitchen bar. A few regulars belly up to the bar. HEATHER sits across from MICKEY in a booth. There's no shortage of tension between them.

> HEATHER
>
> Nice spot you picked here.

> MICKEY
>
> Yeah, well, you know, I figured it was safe.

> HEATHER
>
> Don't flatter yourself, Mickey. I'm just here to talk.

> MICKEY
>
> Okay. Why don't we talk?

> HEATHER
>
> Well, I was thinking about how I treated you a few weeks ago, and I just wanted to apologize. For that and for that night.

> MICKEY
>
> Yeah, well, that was a long time ago, right? It happens.

> HEATHER
>
> So, you think we can be friends?

> MICKEY
>
> Yeah, sure, we can be friends. And I'm sorry too, about bringing up, you know, the whole college tuition payment plan thing, you know?

> HEATHER
>
> It was sort of fun seeing one another again, don't you think?

> MICKEY
>
> I don't know if I'd call it fun. But it was certainly interesting.

HEATHER smiles.

> HEATHER
>
> You know, I've been thinking a lot about you since you came up that day and . . . I don't know . . . I was sort of thinking . . . you know . . . that maybe things could have been different. Maybe we made a mistake.

> MICKEY
>
> We? All I did was come home in the middle of the night to find you and Gorilla Boy in your birthday suits.

> HEATHER
>
> Okay. So I made the mistake . . . but did you have to take off like that, never to be heard from again?

> MICKEY
>
> Yeah. What did you expect me to do, jump in and join the party?

> HEATHER
>
> No. I don't know, maybe give it another chance?

> MICKEY
>
> What . . . and break up this beautiful new friendship? I'm not about to do that. Besides, you know, I'm married now.

An uncomfortable silence. Neither one knows what to do or say next.

> MICKEY
>
> So . . . I'm going to get out of here.

MICKEY stands and walks to the door to leave. HEATHER watches him. MICKEY pauses before exiting and gives HEATHER one last look. He leaves.

◘EXT: BEACH CABANA. DAY

Another day at the beach. MOLLY, RENEE, RON, and CAROL are hanging out on the deck at the cabana.

RON
Your mother told me he's still giving you that down–cycle
nonsense. Thirty-two years your mother and I've been married,
and I don't think we've ever hit a down day, let alone a down
cycle.

RENEE
Mom! Will you just make him go away . . . please!

MOLLY
Yeah, really, Dad, that's disgusting.

RON
What's disgusting? That's true love, young lady.

MOLLY
Please, spare us!

RON
All right, I'm going to spare you. I'm leaving. I know when I'm
not wanted.

RON exits into the cabana.

RENEE

Good! Thank you! And hello? Can we please not talk about my
sex life anymore? Is that possible, please?

MOLLY

Oh, excuse me! But playing with a vibrator does not qualify as
having a sex life.

RENEE

Why does she know that I have a vibrator?

CAROL

She's your sister! Look, honey, maybe you should take him to see
a doctor. It could be physical.

RENEE

All right, look, Mom, don't start with me.

CAROL

Maybe he's having a problem with his—

MOLLY

What kind of problem?

CAROL

You know, getting an erection.

RENEE

Mom, come on! I'm warning you.

CAROL

It's possible.

MOLLY

Maybe he's gay?

RENEE

Francis is not gay.

CAROL

Molly's right.

MOLLY
He could be. You never know.

CAROL
He's always been a bit of a dandy.

RENEE
Excuse me, this is my husband we're talking about here, okay?

RON steps out of the cabana and puts his arm around Renee.

RON
Listen, honey, here's what you do. You go and get yourself some of that Victoria's Secret stuff. It worked for us. If he doesn't want you then . . . then maybe he *is* gay.

RENEE
Okay, Dad, look. My husband is not a homosexual, okay.

RON
Yeah, but he's definitely under suspicion.

RENEE
What are you talking about? What is that supposed to mean, "He's under suspicion"? No . . . this is just a stage!

RENEE escapes into the cabana.

◘ INT: FRANCIS AND RENEE'S BEDROOM. NIGHT

FRANCIS is working on his laptop. RENEE crosses the room and stands at the head of the bed. FRANCIS doesn't look up. RENEE then sits on the bed and takes off her robe, revealing a really sexy nightgown. FRANCIS still does not look up. RENEE slides onto the bed next to FRANCIS and leans on her pillow, offering herself to him. But she gets absolutely no reaction. RENEE gets up and storms back into the bathroom and slams the door. A moment passes. We then hear the buzz of her vibrator. FRANCIS looks up with a shocked expression.

▪ EXT: FRANCIS AND RENEE'S LOFT. DAY

MOLLY and RENEE sit by the window having a cigarette.

> RENEE
> I'm sorry. I looked pretty damn good in that thing, and he barely even looked at me.

> MOLLY
> What did I tell you? He's definitely queer.

> RENEE
> I know. I think you might be right.

> MOLLY
> Call his father and tell him about it. He'll get it out of him.

▪ EXT: MR. FITZPATRICK'S BACKYARD. DAY

FRANCIS and MR. FITZPATRICK sit on the dock.

> MR. FITZPATRICK
> So, are you?

> FRANCIS
> Dad? I told you, I'm in love with another woman. You're my father. How could you say that to me?

> MR. FITZPATRICK
> Listen, Franny, I just wanted to let you know I'm okay with it. If you are or you aren't. It's all right with me. I'll always love you.

> FRANCIS
> Thanks, Dad, but I'm not gay.

▪ EXT: MR. FITZPATRICK'S HOUSE/PORCH. DAY

MICKEY and MR. FITZPATRICK sit on the back patio.

MICKEY

What do you think?

MR. FITZPATRICK

Hell, I don't know. Renee called and told me the story. It sure as hell sounds like he could be. He says he isn't, but you kids are all so fucking nuts it wouldn't surprise me.

MICKEY

I don't think you have to worry about it, Dad. If anyone would know, I would. He's not gay.

MR. FITZPATRICK

Mickey! The kid wears cologne, for Christ's sake!

◘EXT: BASKETBALL COURTS. DAY

FRANCIS and MICKEY sit on a bench, taking a breather after playing hoops.

FRANCIS

Get the hell outta here.

MICKEY

I mean, come on, Fran. You're kind of prissy, all right? You like cooking and clothing and furniture, and I mean, you wear that friggin' cologne, so you know . . .

FRANCIS

Oh, that's brilliant, Mick. That makes me gay?

MICKEY

No, I'm just saying, some people might read you as less than straight. And if you are, you know, I'm your brother and I'll always love you . . . sweet boy.

◘INT: FRANCIS AND RENEE'S LOFT. DAY

We catch FRANCIS and RENEE, still dressed from work, in the middle of a fight. Throughout the scene they run from each other, playing a game of cat and mouse.

FRANCIS

Hold on a second. Just give me a minute here and look at this maleness. How could you possibly think I'm gay?

RENEE

Because you don't look at me anymore, let alone touch me.

FRANCIS

How many times do I have to tell you—

RENEE

If you mention that goddamn down cycle one more time, I swear to God I'll cut that maleness right off. It's just not natural for you not to want to have sex with your wife at least once in the last three months.

FRANCIS

Why is it my fault? Maybe it's your fault. Did you ever think about that?

RENEE

Excuse me? How would this be my fault? I went out there and bought all that lingerie crap and you didn't even look at me.

FRANCIS

Was I not working that night? I'm sorry, do you remember this?

RENEE comes over to FRANCIS, trying to be simpathetic and understanding.

RENEE

Maybe you've got a problem or something. Are you impotent?

FRANCIS

What? No.

Afraid to face her, FRANCIS walks away from RENEE.

RENEE

Maybe you caught some disease or something?

FRANCIS

Yeah, that's it, babe. . . . Syphilis!

Again, RENEE chases him. She puts her hand on his and tries to talk to him.

RENEE

Okay, Francis. Look, honey, if you are a homosexual, you can tell me, okay? I'll understand. I won't be mad. But you've got to talk to me.

FRANCIS

Listen, will you cut it out with the homosexual business? You get me all skieved out every time you say it. Fine. You want to know what's wrong? I'll just come right out and say it . . . just like that. . . . I'll come right out and tell you.

RENEE

Please, I would.

FRANCIS

I'm in love with someone else.
                    (pause)
I want a divorce.

RENEE
(holding back the tears)
What? Since when?

FRANCIS

Just a few months.

RENEE

Who is he?

Again, FRANCIS crosses to the other side of the loft, keeping his back to her.

FRANCIS

Enough with that, okay? It's a she. She's a woman. She's a beautiful, intelligent, sophisticated woman.

RENEE

What does that make me?

FRANCIS

I'm sorry, I didn't mean it like that. It wasn't a comparison.
Don't cry.

*FRANCIS now crosses back to her and tries to comfort her. She brushes off his
touch and grabs her purse off a chair.*

RENEE

I'm not crying. I'm leaving.

RENEE storms out of the apartment.

◘ INT: MOLLY'S APARTMENT. DAY

RENEE, drink in hand, plops down on the couch next to MOLLY.

RENEE
(with tears in her eyes)

He's not gay. He's been seeing another woman, and he wants a
divorce. I need a cigarette.

RENEE grabs the cigarette out of her sister's mouth and takes a long drag.

MOLLY

Well, I guess you can go ahead and send her your vibrator. She's
going to need it.

*RENEE can't help but laugh a bit. MOLLY then puts her arm around
RENEE and gives her a loving hug.*

◘ EXT: CENTRAL PARK WEST. DAY

*MICKEY and HOPE share a summer stroll along the west wall of the park.
The following six scenes will be crosscut.*

HOPE

Your father scares me. I don't think he likes me.

MICKEY

I'm telling you, he likes you, okay? Just the other day he was
telling me how sweet he thinks you are.

◼EXT: MR. FITZPATRICK'S BACKYARD. DAY

MICKEY and MR. FITZPATRICK at the picnic table sharing a few beers.

> MR. FITZPATRICK
> I don't know. There's just something I don't like about her, Mick. She's kind of stuck-up, don't you think?

> MICKEY
> No, not at all. She's just shy with new people, that's all.

◼EXT: CENTRAL PARK WEST. DAY (CONT)

We pick up MICKEY and HOPE where we left them.

> HOPE
> I don't know. He seemed to get upset when I told him I don't talk to my parents anymore.

> MICKEY
> You see? Now I know you're being paranoid, because the guy hated his father and didn't speak to him for years.

◼EXT: MR. FITZPATRICK'S BACKYARD. DAY (CONT)

We also pick up MICKEY and MR. FITZPATRICK where we left them.

> MR. FITZPATRICK
> What kind of person cuts their parents off?

> MICKEY
> I don't know. She says they were really mean.

> MR. FITZPATRICK
> Don't give me that load of horseshit. Nobody was a meaner son of a bitch than my old man, but I was there for him till the day he died.

◘EXT: CENTRAL PARK WEST. DAY (CONT)

Again, we pick up MICK and HOPE walking down the street.

> HOPE
> So he doesn't think I tricked you into this?

> MICKEY
> I mean, granted, he thinks we're nuts, but he said, "As long as you're in love, who cares what anyone thinks?"

◘EXT: MR. FITZPATRICK'S BACKYARD. DAY (CONT)

Picking up where we left off.

> MR. FITZPATRICK
> You didn't give a shit what anyone else thought, did you? You should hear what people are saying.

> MICKEY
> Who? Who's saying anything?

> MR. FITZPATRICK
> Your poor mother thinks you got this girl pregnant. She's just waiting for that announcement.

> MICKEY
> Dad, I knew her for twenty-four hours before we got married, Okay? I didn't have time to get her pregnant.

> MR. FITZPATRICK
> And your brother and I think she's an illegal. She's using you to get a green card.

> MICKEY
> Dad, she's from Vermont.

> MR. FITZPATRICK
> Vermont, my ass. She looks like she's from one of the islands.

MICKEY

Yeah, maybe Rhode Island.

MR. FITZPATRICK

Hey, don't get smart with me, wiseass. You leave this to me. I'm
going to get to the bottom of this one.

◘INT: DeLUCA'S HARDWARE STORE. DAY

*MICKEY and HOPE stand at the counter with MR. DeLUCA, 62, a funny
neighborhood character. DeLUCA is barely tall enough to see over the counter in
his shop.*

MICKEY

Hey, Mr. DeLuca.

DeLUCA

Hey, Mickey, how are you?

MICKEY

Good.

DeLUCA

Come to buy a new drill for your dad's birthday today?

MICKEY

Yeah, how'd you know?

DeLUCA

Your mother was in here this morning. She told me all about it.
She is a fine-looking woman.

MICKEY

Who's a fine-looking woman?

*DeLUCA bags the drill and hands it to MICKEY. HOPE gives MICKEY a
smile. She's enjoying DeLUCA.*

DeLUCA

Your mother. She's beautiful. *Belissima!* Your father doesn't know
how lucky he is. Me, I'm not so lucky. My wife, forty-two years

of marriage, she has no love for me. Oh, well, that's for another time.

> *(pause)*

Hey, how are you going to pay for this?

> MICKEY

Umm. . . . Just put it on the old man's tab, all right? You take care, Mr. DeLuca.

> HOPE

Nice to meet you.

HOPE and MICKEY head out of the store.

> DeLUCA

Ciao. Arrivederci.

> *(calling after them)*

And Mickey . . . say hello to your mother.

◘EXT: FITZPATRICK HOUSE. DAY

MR. FITZPATRICK stands outside the house fighting with his wife, who sits behind the wheel of the family car, a seventies Chevy Suburban. We cannot see MRS. FITZPATRICK'S face or hear what they're saying. FITZPATRICK then raises his hands in surrender as MRS. FITZPATRICK peels away.

FITZPATRICK, pissed off, storms back to the house, kicking a crab trap that stands in his way.

◘INT: FITZPATRICK HOUSE. SAME DAY

MICKEY and HOPE sit at the dining room table in front of their half-eaten meals. FRANCIS stands at the kitchen window watching for his father. FRANCIS then steps back as MR. FITZPATRICK passes the window and steps through the back door. He is not a happy man.

> MR. FITZPATRICK

You are really a jackass, aren't you?

FRANCIS

Dad, I had to tell her.

MR. FITZPATRICK

Yeah, you had to tell her in the middle of my birthday dinner.
Now she's gone off to see Father John. She probably won't be
back here for three weeks. You're going to find my laundry on
your doorstep, buddy.

FRANCIS

Why is she so upset, Dad? She didn't even like Renee.

MR. FITZPATRICK

In case you forgot, moron, as a Catholic you're not supposed to
get divorced.

FRANCIS
(stepping away from his father)

Yeah, you're just supposed to live unhappily and lie to one
another for the rest of your lives.

MR. FITZPATRICK then gets up into FRANCIS'S face.

MR. FITZPATRICK

Hey, wait a minute, buddy. I don't give a shit what you say out
there, but when you're in my house you're not gonna start
bashing the church.

*MR. FITZPATRICK then steps into the dining room and sits down with
MICKEY and HOPE. He pours himself a glass of Jameson and sucks it down.
FRANCIS steps into the doorway and lights a cigarette.*

MICKEY

What are you getting so upset about, Dad? I mean, you don't
even believe in God.

MR. FITZPATRICK

That doesn't mean I stopped being a good Catholic.

*Nobody knows how to respond to that one. MR. FITZPATRICK then grabs
his beer and gets up from the table.*

MR. FITZPATRICK
Excuse me, Hope. I need a moment.

MR. FITZPATRICK exits the room and out the back door.

HOPE
(getting up)
I'm going to go talk to him.

MICKEY
That's not a good idea, Hope.

HOPE shrugs and exits out the back door after MR. FITZPATRICK. FRANCIS then sits down opposite MICKEY.

MICKEY
You had to bring up the divorce during dinner, right?

FRANCIS
Hey, don't blame this all on me, Mick. She was complaining that he spends too much time on the boat anyway. The guy's sixty years old. If he wants to spend the rest of his fucking life on that boat, he should be allowed.

MICKEY
And what about Mom? What should she do, sit at home and wait for him?

FRANCIS
(shrugs)
It's his life, Mick.

◻EXT: MR. FITZPATRICK'S DOCK. SAME DAY

MR. FITZPATRICK stands at the dock overlooking the channel. HOPE walks up and stands next to him.

HOPE
Are you okay?

MR. FITZPATRICK

Yeah.

(pause)

I'm sorry about that in there. Me and the missus haven't been seeing eye to eye these days. Thirty-four years we've been together. I guess things change.

(pause)

So, Mickey tells me you kids are moving to Paris?

HOPE

Yes, I'm going to the Sorbonne.

MR. FITZPATRICK

How come?

HOPE

For my Ph.D.

MR. FITZPATRICK

Ahh. You know, you look French or European. Or . . . um . . . maybe from one of the islands?

HOPE

Oh, yeah? What islands?

MR. FITZPATRICK
Oh, I don't know. . . . So, where *are* you from?

HOPE
Vermont.

MR. FITZPATRICK
Oh. So you're an American citizen then?

HOPE
Yes.

MR. FITZPATRICK
It's funny. Mrs. Fitzpatrick, my wife, when she found out Mickey got married she was understandably upset. She thought it might be some sort of shotgun wedding, seeing as we had never seen you before.

MR. FITZPATRICK waits for a response, HOPE not giving him anything but a knowing smile.

MR. FITZPATRICK
So there's nothing you want to tell me?

HOPE
(enjoying herself)
No.

MR. FITZPATRICK
Because if you are pregnant that's fine. I always thought it might be nice to have a few grandkids running around the house. I thought maybe Franny and Renee might give me a few, but that didn't work out.
(pause)
So, what about you?

HOPE
Thanks, but no. I'm not pregnant.

MR. FITZPATRICK
Good. Good. And you are an American citizen?

HOPE

Yeah. Last time I checked.

MR. FITZPATRICK
(smiling)

Yeah, I thought so.

◘INT: FITZPATRICK HOUSE/KITCHEN. SAME DAY

MICKEY and FRANCIS clear the dining room table of dirty dishes.
FRANCIS runs from kitchen to dining room as MICKEY stays on his heels,
interrogating him.

MICKEY

Tell me where you got it.

FRANCIS

Why?

MICKEY

Francis, just tell me where you got it.

FRANCIS

I told you before, it was a gift.

MICKEY

Yeah, I know that. From who, though?

FRANCIS

What's the big deal? It's a watch.

MICKEY

The big deal is it looks a hell of a lot like a watch I used to own,
okay?

FRANCIS

What does that mean?

MICKEY

Tell me where you got the fucking watch, asshole, all right?

FRANCIS

I don't have to tell you anything.

MICKEY

Listen to me, Francis. That watch on your wrist is my old watch.
When I went to get my TV back from Heather, I gave her the
watch. Now you're wearing the watch. What I want to know is,
why the fuck are you wearing my watch?

FRANCIS

Okay, Heather gave it to me.

MICKEY

No shit, Dick Tracy. What I want to know is why?

FRANCIS

Listen, Mick, it's a long story. I should have told you before but I
didn't know how.

MICKEY

Yeah, you've been having a lot of trouble with that lately, haven't
you?

FRANCIS

The woman I've been seeing . . . is Heather.

MICKEY

My Heather?

FRANCIS

No. My Heather.

MR. FITZPATRICK and HOPE, enjoying a laugh, step into the dining room
through the front door. They stand at the door, listening to the two boys.

MICKEY

You're having sex with my Heather, my ex-fiancée, that bitch
who broke my heart?

FRANCIS

I love her, Mick.

MICKEY

No, you don't.

FRANCIS

Yes, I do.

MICKEY

Let's get this straight, asshole. You don't love my ex-fiancée. Can
you understand that?

HOPE has heard enough. She storms out of the room and up the stairs.

FRANCIS

No, you get this straight. I'm going to marry her, Mick.

MICKEY

What the fuck are you talking about, you're going to marry her?
You don't even know her!

MR. FITZPATRICK then steps in.

MR. FITZPATRICK

Settle down, boys. What the hell is going on here?

MICKEY

You know why this skell is leaving Renee? Because he's
screwing around with Heather, the whore.

FRANCIS

Don't call her a whore.

MICKEY

Hey, I'll call her whatever the fuck I want to call her. You're my
brother. What the hell are you doing?

MR. FITZPATRICK

What do you have to say for yourself, Francis?

FRANCIS

Fuck him. I know why he's really pissed off.

MICKEY
Don't even go there, bitch.

FRANCIS
You know, I should kick your ass for calling my girl a whore.

MICKEY
Now she's your girl? You hear this? This is his girl now.

FRANCIS
Yeah, she's my girl. And I'm gonna kick your fucking ass. What do you think of that, Mr. Loser Cabdriver Who Can't Afford a New TV?

MR. FITZPATRICK grabs the boys before they come to blows. By their collars he drags them out of the house.

MR. FITZPATRICK
All right, ladies, okay. Let's take this outside. Come on.

◻EXT: FITZPATRICK HOUSE/BACKYARD. SAME DAY

HOPE steps out of the back door and onto the porch.

HOPE
I hope you realize how stupid you all look. You're grown men. You're supposed to be brothers.

The three men stand in the middle of the backyard looking at her. The boys are wearing boxing gloves, and MR. FITZPATRICK stands between, serving as the referee.

MR. FITZPATRICK
Sorry, Hope, but sometimes this is the only way you can solve these things.

HOPE shakes her head in disbelief.

MR. FITZPATRICK
(slapping the gloves)
Okay, girls?

MICKEY

I'm not gonna fight you, Franny.

FRANCIS

I know that, Mick. I'm gonna beat you, you're gonna bleed.
Don't worry. It shouldn't take long.

MICKEY

We've got to do this? We have to do this with the gloves and
everything? What are we, in fifth grade again?

FRANCIS

You should have thought of that before you called her a whore,
tough guy.

MR. FITZPATRICK

He's right, Mick. Now, come on. All right, boys, no hitting
below the belt, no kicking, and, Francis, no biting, okay. Let's go.
And may the best man win.

They knock gloves and FRANCIS starts to dance around MICKEY.

FRANCIS

Twenty-five fucking years I've been waiting for the day I'd be
bigger, tougher, stronger than you. When you go down, it's

gonna hurt, baby. I'm gonna kick your fuckin' ass. Are you ready? Are you ready to be humiliated in front of your new wife and father? You are an ugly bitch, I pity you.

Before FRANCIS knows what happened, MICKEY pops him with a shot square in the face. FRANCIS falls straight back. MR. FITZPATRICK looks at MICKEY proudly and puts his arm around him.

> MR. FITZPATRICK
> Good punch, Mick. You always did have a great right.

MICKEY looks over to HOPE. HOPE turns and walks back into the house, pissed. MICKEY follows her. MR. FITZPATRICK then gives a disappointed look to FRANCIS.

> MR. FITZPATRICK
> Come on, Dorothy, it's all over.

◘ INT: MICKEY'S CAB. NIGHT

MICKEY and HOPE ride in silence.

◘ INT: HEATHER'S APARTMENT. SAME NIGHT

HEATHER answers the front door. FRANCIS stands there with a black eye.

> HEATHER
> Hey.

> FRANCIS
> Hey.

> HEATHER
> How are you doing?

HEATHER goes to kiss FRANCIS. He tries to shield his black eye from her but she spots it.

> HEATHER
> *(concerned)*
> What happened to you?

> FRANCIS
> I told Mickey about us.

> HEATHER
> One punch?

> FRANCIS
> It was a cheap shot.

FRANCIS, obviously embarrassed, walks past HEATHER into the apartment.

◼EXT: HOPE'S STREET. SAME NIGHT

HOPE walks quickly down the sidewalk to their apartment. MICKEY follows behind her.

> MICKEY
> Hey, Hope, this had nothing to do with Heather, okay? This had to do with me and Fran. You know he's tried to turn our entire lives into a competition. You know that. This was just another way of him saying, "Fuck you, Mickey, I won."

HOPE stops in front of their building, now face-to-face with MICKEY.

> HOPE
> *(her voice starting to crack)*
> Well, I don't buy it, Mick. Something else was going on there, and you know it.

> MICKEY
> Listen, Hope. I don't know what to tell you, okay? That's what it was about.
> *(pause)*
> I'm going to go take a shower.

MICKEY crosses past HOPE and enters the building, leaving her on the street.

◼ INT: HEATHER'S APARTMENT. SAME NIGHT

HEATHER and FRANCIS sit on a couch in HEATHER'S dark apartment.

> HEATHER
> Does it hurt?

> FRANCIS
> No. No, it doesn't.
> *(pause)*
> I got something for you.

FRANCIS digs into his pocket and pulls out a ring case and hands it to her.

> HEATHER
> What's this?

> FRANCIS
> Will you marry me?

> HEATHER
> You have to get divorced first, Fran.

> FRANCIS
> Yeah, right. Well, this will be like a pre-divorce, pre-engagement, engagement ring. Open it.

She opens it.

> HEATHER
> *(genuinely touched)*
> Oh, Franny. You didn't have to do this. Come here, you poor little thing.

HEATHER touches his face and gives him a kiss.

> FRANCIS
> So?

> HEATHER
> Why are you doing this?

FRANCIS

Because I love you.

HEATHER

Can I have some time to think about it?

FRANCIS

Yeah, I'm not going anywhere.

FRANCIS leans back into the couch.

◘EXT: BAY. EARLY MORNING

MICKEY and MR. FITZPATRICK are out on The Fighting Fitzpatricks *in their favorite fishing spot under the Marine Bay Bridge. MR. FITZPATRICK hands MICKEY a beer and sits down opposite him.*

MR. FITZPATRICK

You know, Mick, I've got to side with Hope on this one. You had no reason to be pissed at Franny.

MICKEY

What, are you kidding me, Dad?

MR. FITZPATRICK

Hey, don't think for a second I can't still knock you on your ass, okay.

MICKEY

Sorry. But, Dad, you know what Fran was up to. My entire life he's been pulling crap like this with me.

MR. FITZPATRICK

Well, let me tell you something. You're no different. You wouldn't have been standing out there in the backyard last night with the gloves on if you were. If you don't believe me, let me refresh your memory. Little League. You're twelve, he's eleven. He's pitching; you're at bat; he's got a full count on his big brother, his idol. If he strikes you out, he's the hero. But what does he do? He throws you a meatball right down the middle. If you take it and go down looking, you make Franny the hero. But you swung away.

MICKEY knows that his father is right. MICKEY then looks out to sea and knows what he has to do.

◻INT: FRENCH CAFE. EVENING

A little French cafe in the Village. HOPE sits alone at a table by the window. She's obviously forlorn. She looks up as MICKEY enters. Slowly and uncertainly, he walks up to her table.

MICKEY

Hey.

HOPE

Hi.

MICKEY sits down opposite her.

MICKEY

So, how we doing?

HOPE

You tell me.

MICKEY

I want to apologize for the other night. I think this whole thing is crazy and stupid. But . . . it's like—you know, I'm a little confused.

HOPE

So how's your friend Heather?

MICKEY

I wouldn't know.

HOPE

Look, Mick, I've been doing some thinking. And who were we kidding? We only knew one another for a few hours. There's no way that was going to work. Right?

MICKEY

I don't know if I'd say that. It's just when you brought up the whole Paris thing it kind of threw me. You know?

HOPE
(starting to get upset)
No, I don't know. You're using that as an excuse. We both know what's really going on here.
(regains her control)
I leave for Paris on Monday, and I think it's best if I go alone.

MICKEY
Are you sure about that?

HOPE
No. But I've made up my mind.

They sit in silence, neither one looking at the other.

◘INT: TORTILLA FLATS. NIGHT

All is quiet before the restaurant opens for business. CONNIE enters from the kitchen and sits with HOPE at a back booth.

CONNIE
What did he say?

HOPE
Not much.

CONNIE
Did he fight for you?

HOPE
No, not really.

CONNIE
What are you going to do about Paris? Go alone?

HOPE
Yeah.

◘ INT: FRANCIS'S LOFT. NIGHT

A knock on the door. FRANCIS answers and MICKEY stands in the doorway.

> MICKEY
>
> Hey, Franny.

> FRANCIS
>
> Hey, Mick, what are you doing here?

> MICKEY
>
> What? I can't come by and see my little brother?

MICKEY walks past him and into the apartment.

◘ INT: FRANCIS'S LOFT. NIGHT (CONT)

FRANNY and MICKEY sit in silence at the kitchen table drinking beers. Finally MICKEY speaks up.

> MICKEY
>
> So, what happened? Out of the thousands of women in Manhattan, you just happen to fall in love with Heather?

> FRANCIS
>
> Listen, Mick, that's not how it happened. We both work on Wall Street. We run in similar circles.

> MICKEY
> *(standing up)*
>
> Jesus, gimme a break, Franny. What do you think, I'm a moron? I'm your brother, man, what were you thinking? You had to go after her, right?

> FRANCIS
>
> It wasn't like that, Mick. Listen, what is your problem anyway? Are you still in love with this woman? Is that why this bothers you?

As MICKEY tears into FRANCIS, he doesn't notice that HEATHER has appeared in the bedroom doorway behind him.

> MICKEY
>
> No, it has nothing to do with that, okay? Listen, we aren't in competition anymore. Look at your life. You won already. You have the big apartment, you've got the nicer clothes, you're Mr. Big Swinging Dick Around Town. . . . I mean, what more do you want?

MICKEY sits back down. HEATHER then speaks up as she enters the room. She is enjoying this.

> HEATHER
>
> Maybe he just wants to be happy.

MICKEY is taken aback. He's having trouble believing what he's seeing and hearing.

> MICKEY
>
> Oh, to be happy? Oh, that's great. Who am I to get in the way of this—what was it?—happiness?

HEATHER steps even closer to the table, playing with her engagement ring.

HEATHER

Franny obviously hasn't told you yet.

MICKEY

Told me what?

HEATHER

Your brother has asked me to marry him.

MICKEY

Great. Terrific. Hey, congratulations.

HEATHER

Thank you.

HEATHER gives MICKEY a cold smile and walks out of the kitchen.

MICKEY

Are you out of your fucking mind?

FRANCIS

Don't start with me, Mick. I love her.

FRANCIS jumps up from the table. MICKEY again chases after him into the living room. They obviously make a habit of this type of behavior.

MICKEY

Hey, no you don't. You don't love her because she's unlovable.

FRANCIS

Oh, so you didn't love her, now?

MICKEY

Yeah, I did, but that was a long time ago and I was a stupid jerkoff who thought he could change her.

FRANCIS

Yeah, well, I don't want to change her.

MICKEY

Yeah, that's because you don't know her.

FRANCIS

Oh, I don't know her? Okay.

MICKEY

Listen, Fran, I didn't want to have to tell you this, but if you are going to marry this girl, there's a lot about her you should know.

FRANCIS

Drop it right here, because there's nothing you can say that's going to change the way I feel about her, okay, Mick?

MICKEY

Listen, Franny, don't be so sure about that. When she was in college, she was . . . she paid her way through school . . . as a call girl.

FRANCIS

What do you mean, a call girl?

MICKEY

I mean you call a service, they send her over, she does her thing—

FRANCIS
(cutting him off)
What do you mean? Like a hooker?

MICKEY

No, not "like" a hooker. She *was* a hooker.

FRANCIS

You are so sick, man. You would stoop to this level.

MICKEY

Francis, you think I would make something like this up?

FRANCIS
(pissed off)
Get the fuck out of here, because the only reason you are saying this is because you don't want me and Heather to be together.

MICKEY
(sincerely)
No. I'm saying this because I'm your brother and I don't want
you to find out after you're married. I'm sorry, man, but it's true.

FRANCIS
(suddenly horrified)
Jesus. A hooker? I knew she was seeing some other guy, but . . .
what the fuck? I can't marry a hooker.

MICKEY
I mean, come on, Franny. It's not that big a deal. It's not like
she's a hooker anymore.

FRANCIS
Not that big a deal? Mick, you're my brother. How could you
keep this from me?

MICKEY doesn't even try to respond to that.

FRANCIS
I gotta . . . I gotta get some air. Tell her . . . tell her . . . I don't
care what you tell her.

*FRANCIS quickly leaves the apartment, slamming the door behind him.
MICKEY sighs and heads back into the kitchen to grab his coat.*

◼ INT: FRANCIS'S LOFT/KITCHEN. NIGHT (CONT)

*MICKEY enters the kitchen as HEATHER reappears. They converge at the
kitchen table. The tension between the two of them builds through the scene.*

HEATHER
Where's Franny?

MICKEY
He's not feeling so good all of a sudden. He went out to get
some air.

HEATHER
You told him?

MICKEY

He is my brother, right?

HEATHER

Yeah, but you always said you didn't have a problem with
that.

MICKEY

I still don't, but if he's going to marry you, I think he's got a
right to know.

HEATHER

Well, I guess we'll see what he's made of.

*They stand, inches apart, looking at each other, neither one sure what to do next
or who's going to do it. They slowly move toward one another as if about to kiss.
HEATHER then leans into him, but reaches past him and grabs his coat off the
chair. She hands it to him. MICKEY shrugs and exits. HEATHER watches
him go.*

◼EXT: MR. FITZPATRICK'S BOAT. DAY

*MR. FITZPATRICK and FATHER JOHN are at the favorite fishing spot,
lines in.*

MR. FITZPATRICK

What the hell are you talking about, Father? She left this
morning saying she was going up there.

FATHER JOHN

I just came from the church. She isn't up there now. In fact, I
haven't seen her at Mass in the past six months.

MR. FITZPATRICK

Hey, John, you better start mixing a little more water with that
wine. She goes to the eight o'clock Mass every morning. She's
up there praying for the boys.

FATHER JOHN

Not in my church she doesn't.

◼EXT: FITZPATRICK HOUSE/PORCH. NIGHT

MICKEY and FRANCIS are sitting on the back porch. MR.
FITZPATRICK, drunk in the kitchen, is breaking plates and making all kinds
of noise. The boys watch him through the kitchen windows.

> MR. FITZPATRICK
> *(screaming)*
> He's lucky I didn't kill him, that little shit.

> MICKEY
> So what's with Dad? He's half in the bag, he's acting crazy, I
> mean . . . what happened today?

> FRANCIS
> Mom left him this morning. She had been going over to
> DeLuca's Hardware Store every day and—I can barely even
> stomach it—screwing around with Mr. DeLuca.

> MICKEY
> Oh, my God, Mom and DeLuca? That's disgusting.

> FRANCIS
> Dad goes up there today and they were in the back room. You
> should have seen it, it was ugly. He gave the little guy a horrible
> beating.

> MR. FITZPATRICK
> *(OS)*
> *(barely audible)*
> Asshole!

> MICKEY
> What about Mom? Where did she go?

> FRANCIS
> She went up to church . . . to pray for Dad.

MR. FITZPATRICK, beer in hand, pops his head through the open kitchen
window.

MR. FITZPATRICK
Pray for me, my ass. She's the one who's gonna need prayers now.

▪ INT: FRANCIS'S PRIVATE CAR. DAY

FRANCIS and TOM, through the streets of Manhattan, again.

FRANCIS
Tommy, do I look as good as I think I do?

TOM
Very handsome, Mr. Fitzpatrick.

FRANCIS
How's the hair, babe?

TOM
Still there, sir.

FRANCIS
It's gonna be a good day, Tom. A good day indeed. First day of
the rest of my life, makin' some changes, babe.

▪ EXT: HEATHER'S APARTMENT. DAY

*FRANCIS and TOM pull up outside Heather's building. FRANCIS jumps
out of the car, flicks his cigarette, and makes his way toward Heather's building.
Just as he is about to enter the lobby, HEATHER heads out the front door with
the doorman, carrying several suitcases.*

FRANCIS
Heather, what's going on here?

HEATHER
I'm leaving.

FRANCIS
No. Forget that. You can't leave. I'm in love with you. I still want
to marry you.

HEATHER

I'm sorry, Francis. Here's your ring. I can't marry you.

*HEATHER hands FRANCIS his ring and makes for the stretch limo that
waits for her. Needless to say, FRANCIS follows.*

FRANCIS

Why not?

HEATHER

Because Papa and I were married this morning.

FRANCIS

What the. . . . One day you say you're going to marry me; the
next you're running off to marry the old man?

HEATHER

He loves me.

FRANCIS

Of course he loves you. You're a beautiful young woman, and
he's got one foot in the grave. This is not because he makes
more money than I do?

HEATHER

No.

FRANCIS

Don't tell me this has anything to do with the sex?

HEATHER

It certainly didn't help matters much. And you know what,
Franny? He didn't care about my past.

FRANCIS

Oh, he doesn't care about your past? Well maybe that's due to
the fact that he doesn't know you were a hooker.

HEATHER

He was my best customer.

HEATHER *smiles and gets into the limo, closing the door in his face. As the car starts to take off, FRANCIS bangs on the window, screaming after her.*

> FRANCIS
> *(yelling)*
> Thanks for the memories! You've ruined my life!

◼ INT: FRANCIS'S OFFICE. DAY

FRANCIS *sits behind his desk, a beaten man. He dials the phone.*

> RENEE
> *(OS)*
> Hello?

> FRANCIS
> Renee?

◼ INT: MOLLY'S APARTMENT. DAY

Crosscut:

RENEE *stands in the living room on the phone.*

> RENEE
> Hello, Francis. What can I do for you?

> FRANCIS
> Listen, this is very hard for me to say, but I feel . . . I know I made a mistake. I know I've been selfish and thoughtless and self-concerned, but I'm going to change. I want the chance to do the right thing. I want you to come home. I miss you. I'm going to pay more attention to you. I want the chance to make it work again. Will you come home?

> RENEE
> *(chuckling to herself)*
> Come on, Francis. What do you want from me here, huh? I don't think so. A day late and a dollar short, you know what I mean?

RENEE walks around the couch and sits down, joining FAT SCOTT, who lies on the couch with a newspaper.

> RENEE
>
> You know, quite honestly, I don't think I can survive another one of your down cycles.

RENEE hangs up the phone and breathes a sigh of relief. FRANCIS hangs up the phone, devastated.

◾INT: TORTILLA FLATS. DAY

A late-summer afternoon. One man sits at the corner of the bar reading the sports pages. CONNIE stands behind the bar, cutting limes. MICKEY steps in and approaches CONNIE.

> MICKEY
>
> Hey, Connie. What's doing?

> CONNIE
> *(not looking up)*
> What are you doing here?

> MICKEY
>
> Um . . . I'm looking for Hope. Is she around?

> CONNIE
>
> No. No, she's not.

> MICKEY
>
> Do you know . . . maybe . . . where she might be? 'Cause I want to talk to her before she goes.

> CONNIE
>
> Look, Mick, you fucked up, all right? You're a jerk. You broke her heart just like I told her you would. Why don't you just get out of here?

> MICKEY
>
> Um . . . do me a favor, though, okay? Tell her that I came by and I want to see her before she goes, okay? And tell her that I miss her.

MICKEY sadly turns and leaves the bar. CONNIE rolls her eyes and heads to the other end of the bar as HOPE walks out of the kitchen toward CONNIE.

                    CONNIE
      Mick was just here.

                    HOPE
      What did he want?

                    CONNIE
      I still say he's a prick, okay? But he did sound upset and he
      did say that he missed you. And he wants to see you before
      you go . . . so maybe you should go by and see him or
      something.

The phone rings. CONNIE grabs it.

                    CONNIE
      Tortilla Flats.

CONNIE listens and nods. She covers the receiver and hands the phone to HOPE.

                    CONNIE
      It's Mick's dad.

Uncertain of what to do, HOPE hesitantly takes the phone.

                    HOPE
      Hello?

◘ INT: McHALE'S BAR. SAME DAY

MICKEY and FRANCIS, now even competitive about their respective misery, sit at the bar drinking pints of Guinness stout. They look like the two self-pitying fools they are.

                    MICKEY
      I blew it. I blew it, man. I had the greatest woman in the world
      and I blew it.

FRANCIS

Hey, you don't know from blowing it, pal. I had the perfect wife
and I screwed it up.

MICKEY

No, you didn't. I had the perfect wife. But you're right . . . you
did screw it up for me, so thanks. I owe you one.

FRANCIS

You know what, Mick? If you really think about it, all this is
entirely your fault.

MICKEY

Oh, really? How do you figure that?

FRANCIS

If you never met and got involved with Heather, where would
we be now?

MICKEY

That's an interesting theory. I hope you didn't hurt yourself
coming up with that one, all-star. I still can't believe you wanted
to marry her. I mean, you are a really confused and demented
soul. It's very upsetting to me as your brother.

FRANCIS

Oh, me confused? Hey, listen, pal, I'm not the fool that's going
to let his new bride enjoy a wonderful honeymoon in Paris
without him.

MICKEY

What do you think, I don't want to go? She said she didn't want
me there, so what am I supposed to do?

FRANCIS

Well, you want to get married without a best man? Pay the
price, pal.

*MICKEY can't help but smile. FRANCIS then takes off his watch and hands
it to MICKEY.*

FRANCIS
Hey, by the way . . . remember, it's six hours ahead over there.

MICKEY looks at the watch and then puts it down on the bar and slides it toward the BARTENDER.

MICKEY
Why don't we give this to the bartender.

◼EXT: FITZPATRICK'S HOUSE. EARLY MORNING

From across the channel, we see FITZPATRICK'S house, dock, and boat. Everything appears peaceful.

◼INT: FITZPATRICK HOUSE/KITCHEN. EARLY MORNING

MR. FITZPATRICK comes into the kitchen from the porch. FRANCIS is having a cigarette while MICKEY sits at the table eating breakfast.

MR. FITZPATRICK
It's going to get nippy out there, boys. And this will probably be our last fishing trip of the season.

FITZPATRICK, his back to the boys, takes a minute and looks out the back window. He turns back around and puts a hand on FRANCIS'S shoulder.

MR. FITZPATRICK
Franny, sit down a second, will ya. I want to talk to you kids.

MR. FITZPATRICK then sits down opposite the two boys.

MR. FITZPATRICK
You know, seeing as we're all sitting here crying in our beers and our women are out living their lives, I would have to say that maybe I should apologize for all the rotten advice I've given you.

FRANCIS
Come on, Dad. You don't have to be so hard on yourself. You don't have to apologize to us.

MR. FITZPATRICK

Yes, I do. But I'm doing this for both of you. Look at you. You're a fucking mess and I'm partly responsible. I don't even know what to tell you. For the first time in my life I'm at a loss for words.

MICKEY

What do you think is going to happen between you and Mom now?

MR. FITZPATRICK

I don't know. We hit a down cycle we just couldn't get out of.

FRANCIS

I told you, it happens.

MR. FITZPATRICK lets out a sigh and softly slaps the table with his hands. There's nothing left to say. He stands.

MR. FITZPATRICK

Hey, but enough of this horseshit. Come on, are we gonna go fishing or what? You know, this isn't going to be so bad, boys. As long as we have each other, we'll do fine.

FRANCIS stands with his father and starts to follow him out to the boat. MR. FITZPATRICK stops and looks back to MICKEY, who is still sitting at the table.

MR. FITZPATRICK
(to Mickey)

Deidre, are you coming?

MICKEY
(standing up)

I don't think I'm going to make it today, Dad.

MR. FITZPATRICK

Why not?

MICKEY

Because Hope's going to Paris tomorrow, and I'm going to go with her.

MR. FITZPATRICK and FRANCIS look to each other. What are you gonna do?

> MR. FITZPATRICK
>
> All right. Well if you can't make it fishing, maybe you can help us load up the gear?

> MICKEY
>
> Yeah.

■EXT: FITZPATRICK'S BACKYARD/DOCK. DAY

MICKEY heads across the backyard and starts down the plank to the dock, carrying the cooler. He stops suddenly and smiles. HOPE, who is sitting in the back of the boat, stands and smiles.

> MICKEY
>
> Hey.

> HOPE
>
> Hi.

> MICKEY
>
> What are you doing here?

> HOPE
>
> I don't know, really. Your dad called to invite me fishing.

MICKEY heads down the plank and stands before her on the dock. He is clearly happy to see her but is still uncertain about what this means.

> MICKEY
>
> Uh, what about Paris?

> HOPE
>
> What about Paris?

> MICKEY
>
> Do you still think you want to go alone?

HOPE
Mick, I didn't come out to Brooklyn this morning to go fishing with your father.

Just then MR. FITZPATRICK and FRANCIS head down the dock, carrying the rest of the gear. FITZPATRICK grabs MICKEY around the shoulder and gives him a hug.

MR. FITZPATRICK
You see, Hope, all his life he's been ignoring my advice. Now he's finally wised up.

MR. FITZPATRICK jumps into the boat as HOPE and MICKEY share a moment. All is well.

MR. FITZPATRICK
(OS)
Come on, Mickey, get your ass in the boat.

HOPE offers MICK a hand and helps him into the boat.

As they head out of the dock and into the channel, FRANCIS stands up at the wheel with his father, while MICKEY and HOPE sit on the stern, arm in arm.

HOPE
Hey, Mr. Fitzpatrick, don't you think I should drive?

MR. FITZPATRICK
(looking over his shoulder)
I think maybe we should take this one step at a time, honey.

They all share a laugh. HOPE then grabs MICKEY and gives him a kiss.

Fade to black.

No Looking Back

Fade in:

◘EXT: A SMALL NORTHEASTERN TOWN.
EARLY MORNING

A blue-collar working-class beach and boating community. It's late winter and it's raining, again.

Credits roll over a montage of early morning in the suburban town: people getting in cars going to work, newspapers being delivered, cops drinking coffee at a diner, old fishermen standing on the docks, a bar being opened with a drunk waiting by the door, etc.

Similar montages will appear throughout the film, the same characters doing the same daily routines.

◘EXT: DINER. MORNING

A small-town diner. Not much happening.

◘INT: DINER. SAME MORNING

TWO GUYS dressed in UPS uniforms get up from their table laughing and head for the door. CLAUDIA, 28, heads from behind the counter and starts to clear their table. One of the guys comes back and throws a dollar bill on a dirty plate.

Thanks, sweetheart.

CLAUDIA looks down at the dollar, wipes it off, sticks it in her pocket, picks it up, and turns away toward the kitchen.

◻EXT: CLAUDIA AND MICHAEL'S HOUSE. LATE AFTERNOON

A shabby little two-family house. An '82 Firebird pulls up in front and CLAUDIA gets out. She grabs the garbage cans from the curb and drags them up the side alley.

◻INT: CLAUDIA AND MICHAEL'S KITCHEN AND DINING ROOM. LATE AFTERNOON

A modest little place. CLAUDIA enters the kitchen and grabs a beer from the fridge. She continues through to the dining room, where her boyfriend, MICHAEL, 28, sits going over some bills.

                    CLAUDIA
Hey, babe.

JOHN CLIFFORD

MICHAEL

Hey. How's it going?

CLAUDIA

Fine.

MICHAEL

How'd you do?

CLAUDIA

Another big day. Seventeen dollars and thirty-two cents.

MICHAEL

Oh, great, that'll help pay the bills.

She puts her money on the table and exits into the bedroom. MICHAEL gets up and follows her.

◼INT: CLAUDIA AND MICHAEL'S BEDROOM. LATE AFTERNOON

MICHAEL

Hey, I'm, gonna go down the street for a few beers. You feel like coming?

CLAUDIA

I don't know. Anybody gonna be there?

MICHAEL

Same as usual. Goldie, Missy, Teresa.

CLAUDIA

All right. Let me just take a quick shower.

MICHAEL

You need any help in there?

CLAUDIA
(laughing)
No. I can manage just fine by myself. Thanks.

MICHAEL
Just yell if you need me.

◼EXT: THE SAND CRAB SALOON. NIGHT

A corner bar. A few dirtbags hanging outside the door smoking. A young couple sucking face on the hood of a car.

◼INT: THE SAND CRAB SALOON. SAME NIGHT

A small neighborhood bar. CLAUDIA sits arm in arm at a back booth with MICHAEL. Across from them sit TERESA, 28, a beauty, and MELISSA, 28, short, pretty, and pregnant. GOLDIE, also known as Adam, 28, shoots pool next to them.

GOLDIE
Hey, Michael, you gonna shoot pool or are you gonna play footsie over there?

MICHAEL
No. What I'm gonna do is kick your ass and take all your money.

MICHAEL grabs his beer, walks over to the pool table, and looks for a shot.

MELISSA then leans in over to CLAUDIA.

MELISSA
So how's your sister doing with the baby?

CLAUDIA
She seems to be okay with it.

TERESA
She ever tell you who the father is?

CLAUDIA
No.

MELISSA
(rubbing her belly)
That's so sad. I can't imagine trying to do this on my own.
Especially at her age. You know, you and Michael really should
think about that, Claudia. You don't want to end up like her and
be almost forty years old before you have your kids.

CLAUDIA
She's only thirty-two, Missy. Besides, what makes you think I
even want kids?

MELISSA
What do you mean you don't want kids? What else would you
do?

CLAUDIA
What else would I do? Oh, I don't know. Maybe try and have
something resembling a life.

MELISSA
What? You don't think that being a mother is having a life?

TERESA
I know what she's waiting for. Claudia still thinks some Prince
Charming is going to stop in the diner one day and sweep her
off her feet and take her off into the sunset or something like
that.

CLAUDIA
Yeah, or at least take me into the city for a nice dinner every
once in a while.

MELISSA
What? You're not happy with Michael?

CLAUDIA
Don't worry, Missy, I'm only kidding.

But a part of her isn't. Before MISSY can respond, MICHAEL calls for her.
CLAUDIA looks off to him as he sets up for a shot.

MICHAEL

Hey, Claudia, this one's for you, babe. Eight ball, corner pocket.

MICHAEL sinks the shot and cheers. He then sticks out his hand and GOLDIE slaps a five-dollar bill into it.

◼ EXT: THE SAND CRAB SALOON. NIGHT

The bar sits on the corner of a residential street. MICHAEL and CLAUDIA step out into the cold night and bundle up, arms wrapped around each other. They say good night to a couple making out on the hood of a car.

◼ EXT: BOARDWALK. NIGHT

An empty boardwalk. CLAUDIA and MICHAEL stand under a streetlight kissing.

MICHAEL

Take a look out there?

CLAUDIA

Yeah?

MICHAEL

What do you think?

CLAUDIA

Think of what?

MICHAEL

The beach?

CLAUDIA

What about it?

MICHAEL

Well, I was thinking that this would be a good spot for the wedding. What do you think?

CLAUDIA

Yeah, it would be nice.

MICHAEL

So? What do you say? Let's decide on a date for this summer.

CLAUDIA

I don't know, Michael. This summer? That seems kind of soon.

MICHAEL

What do you mean you don't know? You don't know if you're ready to do it this summer, or you don't know if you're ready to do it, period?

CLAUDIA

Michael, didn't I already tell you we're gonna get married?

MICHAEL

Yeah.

CLAUDIA

So then what's the hurry? We're not going anywhere. Right?

She puts her arm in his and pulls him close.

MICHAEL

Yeah, but don't keep me waitin' too long. Somebody might come and steal me away.

CLAUDIA

So come on. It's cold out here. Let's go home.

They continue on in silence.

◘EXT: BRIDGE. DAWN

A bus crawls over the bridge and into town.

◘EXT: BUS STATION. EARLY RAINY MORNING

A bus pulls into the empty station and then pulls away. CHARLIE 30, stands on the empty platform with a suitcase. He then heads down the boardwalk.

◘EXT: CHARLIE'S STREET. EARLY MORNING

CHARLIE heads down a narrow street lined with small homes. The beach and boardwalk stand at the end of the block. ALICE, 32, once a beauty but no longer, is grabbing her newspaper off the curb. It's cold outside, and she wears a jacket over her robe. She spots CHARLIE as he heads up the front stoop.

> ALICE
> *(surprised)*

Charlie?

> CHARLIE

Hey, Alice.

> ALICE

What's with the bag? You moving back home or something?

> CHARLIE

No, just here for a little visit.

> ALICE

Oh, yeah?
> *(heads back up stoop)*
Well, you just make sure you find time to come on over for a drink before you go, all right?

> CHARLIE

Yeah, sure.

CHARLIE crosses the lawn to a small winterized two-story bungalow. An old '72 Pontiac LeMans sits on blocks in the driveway. CHARLIE turns and looks out at the street. He is not happy to be home. He turns and enters the house.

◻INT: CHARLIE'S MOM'S HOUSE. MORNING

CHARLIE heads straight up the stairs.

◻INT: CHARLIE'S MOM'S HALLWAY. MORNING

CHARLIE takes off his wet jacket.

> CHARLIE
> Hey Mom, you home?

> MOM
> (OS)
> I'm in here.

◻INT: CHARLIE'S MOM'S BEDROOM. MORNING

MOM, 53, a tired woman wearing a cleaning woman's uniform, appears at Charlie's door.

> MOM
> I guess you got the check I sent.

> CHARLIE
> Yeah, I'll pay you back in a few weeks.

> MOM
> I won't hold my breath. This just a friendly visit, or are you home for good?

> CHARLIE
> No . . . just a visit.

> MOM
> What happened, fired again?

> CHARLIE
> No, I quit.

MOM
(exiting past him)
Oh, good for you. Listen, I'm not gonna stand for any of your
bullshit this time, Charles. The last three years have been very
peaceful around here without you. So you'll act like an adult or
you'll be out on your ass. Understand? And get that goddamn
car off my lawn, too.

CHARLIE nods and watches her go down the stairs. He closes his bedroom door.

MOM
(yelling from the stairs)
And don't touch any of my beers either.

◘ INT: CLAUDIA'S MOM'S HOUSE. DAY

*CLAUDIA steps through the front door carrying grocery bags and heads in
through the living room. Claudia's sister, KELLY, thirty-two years old, still sexy
but has seen better days, is sitting on the couch watching TV with a baby in her
arms.*

CLAUDIA
Hey, Kelly.

KELLY
Hey, babe. What's up? You need a hand?

CLAUDIA
No, I got it. Mom up yet?

KELLY
Yeah, she's right there in the kitchen.

◘ INT: CLAUDIA'S MOM'S KITCHEN. DAY

*CLAUDIA enters the kitchen and KELLY follows, carrying her child. MOM,
63, is at the kitchen table, chain smoking.*

MOM
Oh, Claudia, I told you you don't have to do that. I can go to
the store myself, you know.

CLAUDIA gives her mom a kiss and starts to put away the groceries. She puts a carton of butts down in front of her.

> CLAUDIA
>
> Ah, come on, Mom, don't worry about it. So what's going on, Kelly? Anything happening?

> KELLY
>
> Same shit, different day.

> MOM
>
> She can't find a date.

> KELLY
>
> You should talk, Mom. At least I get out of the house every once in a while.

> CLAUDIA
>
> What about that guy Marty I told you about? I figured he'd be right up your alley.

> KELLY
>
> The guy from the fish store? No thanks. Do I really look that desperate to you?

> MOM
>
> Do you want us to honestly answer that?

KELLY smiles and gives MOM the finger as she turns her back.

> MOM
>
> So no news from your father, I guess.

> CLAUDIA
>
> Don't you think you'd be the first one I'd tell if I heard from him?

> KELLY
>
> Mom, please don't start with that again.

> MOM
>
> Start with what?

KELLY

He left Ma. He ain't coming back. Trust me, I know something about guys like that.

MOM

Why would you say that? I told you he did this when you were just a baby, but he came back then, didn't he?

KELLY

If he really gave a shit about us, he would've at least called already. Besides, I wouldn't even talk to the son of a bitch now if he did call.

MOM

Watch your mouth, Kelly. He's still your father.

KELLY

Not as far as I'm concerned. And why don't you take this fucking thing off the wall already.

KELLY points to a framed picture of their father in his navy uniform as she exits. CLAUDIA sighs, turns, and goes back to the groceries. MOM lights another butt.

◻INT: CLAUDIA AND MICHAEL'S LIVING ROOM. DUSK

MICHAEL and CLAUDIA sit on the couch in front of the TV. MICHAEL eats his dinner while CLAUDIA looks through a fashion magazine and then looks at MICHAEL.

MICHAEL
(to food)
Hey, this is pretty good. I think you're finally getting the hang of it.

CLAUDIA smiles and goes back to her magazine. MICHAEL puts down his fork and slides up next to her.

MICHAEL
What's wrong, babe?

CLAUDIA

It's my mom. She just won't give up hope and it's tough to watch, you know?

MICHAEL

I still don't get your dad. I don't get how a guy can run off on his wife and kids like that.

CLAUDIA

Yeah. But . . . I think I can sort of understand why he left.

MICHAEL

You can?

CLAUDIA

Yeah. I mean, he obviously wasn't happy anymore.

MICHAEL

Big fucking deal. Where is it written that we're supposed to be happy all the time? If you have a family, you suck it up and you do the right thing. You don't run off like some coward.

CLAUDIA

He didn't love my mother anymore. What was he supposed to do, spend the rest of his life being miserable?

MICHAEL

That's not the point. How does a guy abandon his wife like that? Leaves in the middle of the night, no explanation? If he didn't love her anymore, he should have told her and asked for a divorce.

CLAUDIA

He tried. But you know my mother, she just didn't want to hear it. She wouldn't believe it.

MICHAEL

That's bullshit. And why the hell are you defending him? You don't see how this has affected your mother? The woman hasn't left the house in six months.

CLAUDIA

I'm not defending him. I hate the son of a bitch for what he's done to her. But he is my father and I grew up in that house, so I can sort of understand his side.

MICHAEL

Well, I can't.

MICHAEL *stands and grabs his plate. He looks at her as if he doesn't know her and then exits.*

CLAUDIA
(to herself)
I wouldn't expect you to.

◘INT: PIZZA PLACE. DAY

CHARLIE *stands at the counter.* TONY, 28, *pulls two slices out of the oven and hands them to* CHARLIE.

TONY

So what happened? California didn't work out?

CHARLIE

No. It wasn't that. It was just . . . I don't know. I figured I should come back east, check up on my mom, you know, before, you know, she's getting old and everything, so . . .

TONY

Yeah, I know. My old man's getting sick now too. So what's it like out there? Nice weather, though, there, right?

CHARLIE

Yeah, it was all right.

TONY

A lot of good-looking babes, I bet, fucking hanging out in bikinis and shit all the time, right?

CHARLIE

Yeah, and they're all gorgeous. Not like the skanks here. You know, you gotta go out there sometime instead of holing up in this place all your life.

> TONY

Yeah, you're right, you know, I should. But I told you, my pop's sick now, and John went to college, so I'm stuck here running the place. So, what are you gonna do? So, I guess you heard about Michael and Claudia already?

> CHARLIE

No. Why? What happened?

> TONY

Nothing happened. I just figured you would've heard already.

> CHARLIE

What the hell are you talking about? Would've heard what?

> TONY

Oh, man.
> *(hesitates)*
Take a look behind you.

CHARLIE turns and looks out the window. His POV:

◘EXT: MAIN STREET. DAY

CLAUDIA exits a store across the street and is greeted by MICHAEL. They kiss.

CLAUDIA looks up and sees CHARLIE in the pizza place. She gets in the car and they take off.

◘INT: PIZZA PLACE. DAY

CHARLIE is pissed.

> TONY

What do you think?

CHARLIE

I could care less.

◘INT: THE SAND CRAB SALOON. NIGHT

MELISSA, GOLDIE, TERESA, CLAUDIA, and MICHAEL stand around the pool table having a few beers. MICHAEL and GOLDIE are still dressed from work.

GOLDIE

When did you hear about this?

CLAUDIA

This afternoon at the diner. Alice Smith told me.

MELISSA

Who's Alice Smith?

TERESA

You know her. She's the slut that lives across the street from him.

GOLDIE

Hey, don't hold that against her. As far as I'm concerned there aren't enough girls like her around these days.

MELISSA gives him a playful slap to the head. They all laugh.

GOLDIE

I can't believe he hasn't called us yet. Has he called you yet?

MICHAEL

No.

GOLDIE

I wonder if he's home for good. Did she say if he was home for good?

CLAUDIA

We really didn't talk about it, Goldie. She just asked me if I knew he was home, that's it.

MELISSA

Does he know about you guys?

CLAUDIA

I have no idea.

GOLDIE

You think he'd be pissed?

MICHAEL

Who gives a shit what he thinks?

GOLDIE

Come on, Mikey, you've known the guy since the first grade, why don't you give him a break already, you know.

MICHAEL

Are you kidding me? The guy's a mutt and always has been. I'm sure he's still out trying to bang any skank he can get his hands on.

TERESA

You sound jealous.

MICHAEL

Jealous? You kidding me? If anything I feel bad for the poor bastard.

GOLDIE

He's thirty years old and single. I mean, come on, I'd do the same thing if I was him.

MELISSA *gives GOLDIE another playful smack.*

GOLDIE

I said if I was single. Besides, we haven't seen the guy in three years. Maybe he's changed.

MICHAEL

Yeah, I should hope so. For his sake.

GOLDIE

Well, even so, somebody should tell him. Now, I could tell him
if you want me to, or you could tell him.

MICHAEL

I could give two shits who tells him. You want to tell him, you
tell him.

GOLDIE

I think one of us should tell him before he hears it from
somebody else, don't you? What do you think, Claudia?

All eyes are on CLAUDIA.

CLAUDIA

Yeah, probably.

GOLDIE

Maybe I'll stop by his house tomorrow and see him. You should
probably come with me, don't you think?

MICHAEL

Fine. You want me to tell him, I'll tell him. You happy now, you
little pain in the ass?

GOLDIE

I just think it's the right thing to do.

MICHAEL

Well, congratulations for you, Huck Finn. Hey, Teresa, let me
get another beer, will ya?

GOLDIE nods. MICHAEL walks away. CLAUDIA shrugs.

◘EXT: CHARLIE'S STREET. DUSK

*FITZY and some other young teens are hanging out in the street, drinking beer
and smoking. MICHAEL pulls up and parks his beat-up '71 Impala in front of
Charlie's house. He gets out.*

KIDS

Hey, nice car.

MICHAEL

Yeah, and make sure you scumbags keep your hands away from it, okay.

The kids say nothing. MICHAEL heads up Charlie's front porch and without hesitation rings the bell.

▪ INT: CHARLIE'S BEDROOM. DUSK

CHARLIE sits on his bed watching TV. Off screen we hear his mother yell for him to get the front door. He slowly climbs out of bed and exits.

▪ EXT: CHARLIE'S MOM'S FRONT PORCH. DUSK

MICHAEL stands on Charlie's Mom's front porch knocking on the door. CHARLIE opens the door and they stand there talking. It's clear from the get-go, these guys don't like each other.

CHARLIE

Hey, Michael, how's it going?

MICHAEL

What do you mean how's it going? I hear you've been home for a week and nobody gets a call?

CHARLIE

You know, I was gonna call you guys, but . . . I just figured I'd run into you at the bar sooner or later. So what's up?

MICHAEL

Nothing. I heard you were home so I figured I'd stop by and say hello.
(pause)
So you gonna invite me in or are we gonna stand out here and freeze our asses off?

CHARLIE
Yeah. Come on in.

CHARLIE opens the door and lets Michael by.

◘INT: CHARLIE'S MOM'S HOUSE. NIGHT

CHARLIE and MICHAEL walk through the living room. CHARLIE'S MOM is sitting on the couch. MICHAEL says hello and barely gets one back. They head to the kitchen.

◘INT: CHARLIE'S MOM'S KITCHEN. NIGHT

CHARLIE and MICHAEL sit at the table with beers.

CHARLIE
Everything all right?

MICHAEL
Yeah. Everything's fine.
(looking around kitchen)
Place hasn't changed much.

CHARLIE
Yeah, well my mother hasn't gotten around to hiring a new interior decorator just yet.

MICHAEL barely laughs.

MICHAEL
So how you doing?

CHARLIE
I'm doing good.

MICHAEL
I saw the LeMans out in the driveway. You got that back up and running?

CHARLIE

I'm trying to. I feel for you, though. I see you still got the Impala. I can't believe that thing is still on the road.

MICHAEL

Yeah. Well after you left, I finally got a decent mechanic.
(pause)
So what brings you back. You miss home or something?

CHARLIE

Did I miss home? What? Is there something here to miss?

MICHAEL

So what's the occasion, then? You just home for a vacation?

CHARLIE

No. Just figured I should come home, check up on my mom. You know? Figure I'll try and save a little money while I'm here and then probably take off after that.

MICHAEL

Oh, yeah? So you got a job lined up here all ready?

CHARLIE

Yeah, Bugsy's giving me a couple of days at the station, pumping gas.

MICHAEL

That's real good. So, you seen anybody else since you been back?

CHARLIE

No. I'm actually hoping to maybe run into Claudia if she's still around. You know I wouldn't mind starting that up again.

MICHAEL

Listen, Charlie, that's what I wanted to talk to you about.

CHARLIE

What's up? Don't tell me she's married.

MICHAEL

No, not exactly but . . . you see, me and Claudia are together now.

CHARLIE

What do you mean, together?

MICHAEL

I mean, we're together, living together. Probably even gonna get married this summer.

CHARLIE

No shit. How long has that been going on?

MICHAEL

About three years now.

CHARLIE

Three years? You didn't waste any fucking time, did you?

MICHAEL

You treated her like shit and then you took off. I treat her good.

CHARLIE

You and Claudia? I never would've thought that. That's good, though. That's real good. So you guys engaged or something?

MICHAEL

Basically.

CHARLIE

What do you mean basically? How is one basically engaged?

MICHAEL

We've both agreed we're gonna get married, but we haven't decided on a date yet so, yeah, I guess we're not officially engaged then.

CHARLIE

That's great, man. Listen, seriously, no bullshit, I'm happy for you.

                    MICHAEL
So you're cool with this?

                    CHARLIE
Michael, come on. You and me been friends for too long to let
some fucking chick get in the way of that. Right? Even if it is
Claudia.

                    MICHAEL
Well, she's not just some fucking chick, but I get what you're
saying. So I'm not gonna have to deal with any classic Charlie
bullshit then?

                    CHARLIE
No. Me and her were over a long time ago.

                    MICHAEL
Yeah, a long time ago. So, no hard feelings, right?

MICHAEL raises his glass and CHARLIE hesitates. They toast.

                    CHARLIE
Of course, man. And to old friends.

◘INT: CLAUDIA AND MICHAEL'S LIVING ROOM. NIGHT

*CLAUDIA irons some clothing. She checks her watch. She hears a car pull up.
She plays it cool. MICHAEL enters and stands at the doorway.*

                    MICHAEL
Freezing out there tonight.

                    CLAUDIA
So? How'd it go?

                    MICHAEL
What?

                    CLAUDIA
What? Did you go see him?

MICHAEL

Yeah.

CLAUDIA

And?

MICHAEL

He's still an asshole.
(beat)
He's working back at the gas station pumping gas. Really setting the world on fire.

MICHAEL enters the bathroom and closes the door. CLAUDIA stands outside.

CLAUDIA

Did you tell him about us?

MICHAEL
(OS)

Yep.

CLAUDIA

How did he react?

MICHAEL
(OS)

He seemed to be okay about it.

CLAUDIA
(somewhat disappointed)

Good.

◼ EXT: BOARDWALK. DAY

All is quiet except for a stray dog.

◼ INT: CLAUDIA AND MICHAEL'S KITCHEN. DAY

MICHAEL opens the fridge door and grabs the milk. He tries to pour it into his coffee but it's empty.

MICHAEL

Hey, Claudia!

Crosscut:

◼ INT: CLAUDIA AND MICHAEL'S BEDROOM. DAY

CLAUDIA stands in the bedroom getting dressed. She checks herself out in the mirror and exits. She looks great. She throws on some perfume. They yell back and forth to one another.

CLAUDIA

Yeah?

MICHAEL

I thought you said you were gonna go to the store?

CLAUDIA

I did.

MICHAEL

You forgot to get the milk then.
(to himself)
And I can't have a cup of coffee without the milk, can I?

CLAUDIA sighs and checks herself one more time. She exits.

◼ INT: CLAUDIA AND MICHAEL'S KITCHEN. DAY

MICHAEL sits at the table going over bills and drinking his black coffee. CLAUDIA enters.

CLAUDIA

There's no milk?

MICHAEL holds up the empty container. He's trying hard not to be an asshole about it.

CLAUDIA

Okay. Well, I'm running out. I'll pick some up before I come home then.

MICHAEL

Where are you running out that you got all dolled up for?

CLAUDIA

What do you mean, all dolled up? I'm not dolled up.

MICHAEL

Yeah, you are. Look at you. You going someplace special or something?

CLAUDIA

No. Just going over to check on my mom and then do some shopping.

MICHAEL

Oh, yeah. Well, I don't have to be at work till six. Give me a few minutes and I'll go with you?

CLAUDIA

No, no, that's okay. I'm just gonna go by and see if she needs anything. Okay? I'll see you later.

She blows him a kiss and exits. MICHAEL watches her suspiciously.

◘ EXT: CLAUDIA AND MICHAEL'S DRIVEWAY. DAY

CLAUDIA steps out of her house and into her car. She checks herself in the mirror. She pulls away.

◘ EXT: BUGSY'S GAS STATION. DAY

CHARLIE and THE FOOT, 42, a scruffy gas jock with a club foot, stand in the door of the garage drinking coffee. It's a cold windy day. CLAUDIA pulls up at one of the pumps. CHARLIE casually walks over to her car and leans down by the passenger-side window.

CHARLIE

I was wondering when you'd find the time to stop by and say hello.

CLAUDIA

Hey, Charlie.

She smiles. They are happy to see each other.

CLAUDIA

How you doing?

CHARLIE

Same old, same old. What's up? You need some gas?

CLAUDIA

Yeah. Fill it up, regular.

CHARLIE smiles at her again and goes around back and starts to fill the car. He comes back around to the driver's side door and leans in.

CHARLIE

So what did you do to yourself, you get a haircut or something?

CLAUDIA

Charlie, it's been over three years. I got a lot of haircuts since then.

CHARLIE

No, I know. I was just thinking you just look . . . I don't know, you know . . . you look nice. I figured maybe you got a haircut or something. I don't fucking know.

CLAUDIA
(somewhat charmed)
Thanks. Look, I wanted to talk to you. Can we go somewhere to talk?

CHARLIE

Is everything all right?

CLAUDIA

Yeah. Everything's fine. I just want to talk. Can you get a few minutes?

CHARLIE
Yeah, sure. Don't worry about it.

◼EXT: BOARDWALK. DAY

CLAUDIA and CHARLIE walk along the quiet boardwalk.

CHARLIE
Been awhile since we walked down here. We got some good
memories on this beach, don't we?

CLAUDIA
Yeah. And plenty of bad ones too.

CHARLIE
Somehow I manage to forget about those. You know, block all
that crap out.

CLAUDIA
Well, that's convenient.
(beat)
So, does it feel good to be home?

CHARLIE
Not really. Feels good to see you, though. I missed you, you
know.

CLAUDIA
Oh, you missed me, did you? Not enough to pick up the phone,
though, huh?

CHARLIE
That's not true. I almost called a couple of times, but you know,
I figured you didn't want to hear from me.

CLAUDIA
Yeah, it's probably just as well.
(pause)
So I guess you spoke to Michael?

CHARLIE

Yeah. He came by the house. That was really nice of him to deliver the good news himself.

CLAUDIA

I'm sorry. I thought I should be the one to tell you but Michael insisted. He said you weren't mad.

CHARLIE

Of course I'm not mad. Who wouldn't be thrilled to find out that one of their best friends is now engaged to their ex-girlfriend? Shit, I wanted to throw a party for you two.

CLAUDIA

Oh, yeah. Well you can imagine how excited I was three years ago to show up at your house after I got out of the hospital to have your mother tell me that you'd moved to California.

CHARLIE

Hey. It's not like I ran out on you. Remember. We broke up before that, all right? But you and Michael is a different story. I mean, I think I got good reason to be a little pissed off here.

CLAUDIA

Give me a break, Charlie. It's not like you and him were ever actually the best of friends.

CHARLIE

Well, that's real obvious now, ain't it?

CLAUDIA

Hey, at least he treats me nice, which is a hell of a lot more than I could ever say for you.

CHARLIE

No shit he treats you nice, you're the best thing he's ever got his hands on. I'm just surprised you would settle for that. So what are you gonna do, end up like his sisters? Fat-assed housewives eating themselves to death every Sunday over at his mother's house?

CLAUDIA
(starting to get upset)

No.

CHARLIE

Then what is it then? His old man die and leave him a pile of
money?

CLAUDIA

No. He's just a good guy and he loves me.

CHARLIE

Of course he loves you. The guy's had a hard-on for you since
sixth grade. Only you never used to give him the time of day.
Now you're probably cleaning his fucking dirty underwear. I
swear, it's really been a couple of friggin' banner years for you
since then, hasn't it? Working at the shitbag diner and dating the
back-stabbing bastard. Your dreams are really coming true here,
huh?

CLAUDIA

Who do you think you are? What is so great about your
miserable life that you're gonna criticize me? Big deal, you ran
off to California. But it looks to me like you're right back where
you started, aren't you?

CHARLIE

No, see, that's where you're wrong. I'm only here for a short
visit. This shit ain't my life.

CLAUDIA

Oh, really? You're back living at home and working the same
job you had in high school. Take a look at yourself, Charlie. You
been talking "this shit" for a long time. And you know what? It
looks like "this shit" is all you got.

*CLAUDIA turns and walks away from him. CHARLIE is somewhat taken
aback. She gets into her car.*

◾EXT: CLAUDIA AND MICHAEL'S HOUSE. DUSK

CLAUDIA drags the garbage cans up the side alley and enters her house.

◾EXT: STREET. DAY

CLAUDIA and KELLY stroll through the street.

> CLAUDIA
>
> Mom seems to be doin' okay. How's she holding up?

> KELLY
>
> Oh, she's great. Smoking and drinking herself to death every day, and then she tells me I need to get out and exercise more often.

> CLAUDIA
> *(kidding)*
>
> She might have a point there, Kelly. You are getting a little bit of a fat ass.

> KELLY
>
> Hey sweetheart, I'm a thirty-five-year-old single mother still living at home. I got bigger problems than worrying about the size of my ass. You know?

> CLAUDIA
>
> So then why don't you let me help you out once in a while? I told you I'd watch the baby any time you need.

> KELLY
>
> I don't know if I need any more of your help. Thanks to you, every time I go into the fish market, Marty is drooling all over me.

> CLAUDIA
>
> What about that cop from Breezy?

> KELLY
>
> Didn't work out. But you know what happens, the minute you bring up marriage, they head for the fucking hills. I swear, the

◾ 251 ◾

only guys I meet that want to get married are the ones I meet down at unemployment.

CLAUDIA

You see, with me and Michael it's just the opposite. He's dying to get married, have kids, and do the whole mom and pop thing.

KELLY

And you want to screw some other guys before you settle down and start squeezing out Mikey Juniors?

CLAUDIA
(joking)

Mikey Juniors? No, it's not that. I'm just afraid that if I marry him then that will be it. And I'll spend the rest of my life doing his laundry, making his dinner, and spending every weekend at his mother's house, listening to her tell me what a horrible wife I am.

KELLY

So if you feel that way, why did you tell him you'd marry him?

CLAUDIA

Honestly, I don't know. What else am I really gonna do, you know, all of sudden go to college or something? I don't think so. Besides, he's a good guy and he's good to me. And everybody kept telling me I should marry him already, so I told him I would.

KELLY

That's bullshit, Claudia. You got to do what's right for you, not what's right for everybody else.

CLAUDIA

You don't understand, though. If I were to say no to him now, it would kill him.

KELLY

I don't know what else to tell you, babe. Nobody said this shit was easy.

CLAUDIA

Yeah, but I don't remember anybody saying it would be this
hard, either, did they?

The two women sit there.

◘INT: DINER. RAINY DAY

*CLAUDIA and an OLDER WAITRESS stand behind the counter. The diner
is all but empty.*

CLAUDIA

Ugly day out there, ain't it?

OLDER WAITRESS

Story of my life.

*The OLDER WAITRESS gets up and walks down to give a refill to a cop at
the end of the counter.*

◘EXT: DINER. RAINY DAY

*CHARLIE steps from a beat-up old Buick tow truck. The door of the truck
reads* BUGSY'S GARAGE. *He climbs out and enters the diner.*

◼INT: DINER. RAINY DAY

CLAUDIA sees him and shakes her head. CHARLIE walks in, smiles, and heads down to a booth near the window.

CLAUDIA finishes with the other customer and brings some coffee to CHARLIE. She's not happy to see him.

> CLAUDIA
>
> You here to eat?

> CHARLIE
>
> Yeah.

> CLAUDIA
>
> You know what you want or you need a menu?

> CHARLIE
>
> Yeah, let me get a cheeseburger, medium rare, with some fries.

> CLAUDIA
>
> That's it?

> CHARLIE
>
> No. There's actually something I want to ask you. Can you sit down with me a second?

> CLAUDIA
>
> You can't see I'm working here?

> CHARLIE
>
> Hey. Come on. It's not like they're gonna fire you. You're the only goddamn waitress in this place with a pulse. Come on, look, I'm sorry about the other day at the beach. Just sit down with me a second. I'm not gonna bite you.

CLAUDIA looks over her shoulder at the OLDER WAITRESS. She is smoking a butt, leaning across the counter, and flirting with the cop. CLAUDIA sits.

CLAUDIA

So?

CHARLIE

So . . . look, I'm sorry about the other day. I was being an asshole.

CLAUDIA

That's what you wanted to ask me?

CHARLIE

No. Look, I've been doing some thinking since I saw you and . . . I mean, I wanted to know if you're happy with this? You know, living here, being a waitress, your whole routine?

CLAUDIA

What business is that of yours?

CHARLIE

Come on, Claudia. I've known you your whole life. I just can't buy that you're okay with this.

CLAUDIA

Well, it's not like I'm planning on being here forever, you know.

CHARLIE

You see that old bag over there? That's what she said too. Now look at her. Another couple of months here, and your hair is gonna turn blue too.

CLAUDIA laughs.

CLAUDIA

Did you come here to eat or to abuse me?

CHARLIE reaches across the table and grabs her hands. CLAUDIA quickly pulls away.

CHARLIE

What happened to all those things you said you were gonna do?
Remember what I used to call you? "Cloudia," 'cause you
always had your head in the clouds? Always talking about
getting outta here, seeing some of the world. What happened to
all that?

CLAUDIA
(pulling her hands away)
I was eighteen years old and I grew up. That's what happened.

CHARLIE

I don't buy that.

CLAUDIA

What makes you think I care what you buy? Besides, what about
you? Of the two of us, you were the one with big plans, the big
dreams. What happened to you?

CHARLIE

I didn't give up. It just didn't work out this time. But at least I
gave it a shot. I got out of here. And I'm gonna be back out
there giving it another shot in a month or so.

CLAUDIA

So why did you even bother coming back home?

CHARLIE

Honestly? To see you.

CLAUDIA laughs.

CLAUDIA

Hey. Well, here I am in all my glory. Now what are you gonna
do?

CHARLIE

Well, that's what I wanted to talk to you about. I mean, I'm
thinking if you're not really that happy here, then maybe when I
take off again in a month or so, you could come with me like
we always planned.

CLAUDIA

Oh, sure, just like that. We'll take off together, no big deal. First
of all, I never said I wasn't happy, you did. Second of all, we've
been through this once before, Charlie. Only we were kids then,
and that's why it seemed romantic. But now, it don't seem so
romantic, you know?

CHARLIE

Why? Because of Michael?

CLAUDIA

Partly. And because I don't trust you anymore. Remember, you
have a habit of running away when things get a little ugly.

CHARLIE

What are you talking about?
(whispering)
Are you talking about the abortion?

CLAUDIA

Yeah.
(mocking his whisper)
I'm talking about the abortion.

CHARLIE

Hey, I stayed and made sure everything was okay before I left. I
even talked to the doctor.

CLAUDIA

Oh, you talked to the doctor? That was mighty big of you. Yeah
well, you know what, everything wasn't okay. And I needed you
and you were gone.

CHARLIE

What wasn't okay?

CLAUDIA

It doesn't matter now. But to answer your question, no, I don't
want to go anywhere with you.

CHARLIE seems crushed by this. Claudia stands.

CHARLIE
So what are you gonna do? You're really gonna marry Michael?

CLAUDIA
Yeah.

CHARLIE
I don't see a ring.

CLAUDIA
Don't worry. It's coming.

CHARLIE
Well. I guess you play the cards you're dealt, right?

CLAUDIA
Yeah, or sometimes you just run away.
(she gets up from the table)
Listen, I'm gonna get back to work now. Please just leave me alone, okay.

CHARLIE nods and watches CLAUDIA get up and walk into the kitchen.

◘EXT: CLAUDIA AND MICHAEL'S DRIVEWAY. RAINY NIGHT

CLAUDIA pulls her car up into the driveway and turns off the radio. She sits and stares at the wipers going back and forth.

◘INT: CLAUDIA AND MICHAEL'S BEDROOM. NIGHT

CLAUDIA is in bed with the TV on. We hear MICHAEL come in the house. CLAUDIA clicks off the TV and closes her eyes and rolls over. MICHAEL enters the room and stands at the foot of the bed while getting undressed. The room is cold.

MICHAEL
Freezing in here. The heat out again?

CLAUDIA
(mumbling)
I don't know. I guess so.

MICHAEL
You asleep?

CLAUDIA
No. Not really.

MICHAEL
Sorry I'm a little late. I stopped over at Goldie's on my way
home. He wanted to show me the sonogram Missy had done
this week. Did you get to see it yet?

CLAUDIA
No.

MICHAEL
It was pretty cool. It's gonna be a boy. You can already see his
little pecker.

CLAUDIA
(disinterested)
Really?

MICHAEL
What do you think we'll have first, a boy or a girl?

CLAUDIA
I don't know.

MICHAEL
I think I'd like a boy first. A guarantee to carry on the family
name, you know?

CLAUDIA nods and tries to smile.

MICHAEL
You know, babe, you're gonna make a great mother.

MICHAEL heads into the bathroom.

◼EXT: THE TOWN. DAWN

Montage of the town. All is quiet: an empty boardwalk, garbage being collected at The Sand Crab, Claudia's street empty and wet.

◼EXT: CLAUDIA AND MICHAEL'S HOUSE. DAWN

MICHAEL steps out of the house and into his car. The window's covered with frost. He turns the key. The car doesn't start.

> MICHAEL
> Ah, come on, you bastard. Not again.

He drops his head into his hands, a beaten man.

◼INT: BUGSY'S GARAGE. NIGHT

Late night. The garage part of the station is closed for the night except for one bay. The rest of the garage is dark. CHARLIE works under his car on the lift. MICHAEL stands beside him.

> CHARLIE
> So what happened to your other mechanic?

> MICHAEL
> He died.

> CHARLIE
> Look, Michael, I don't want you to take this the wrong way, but that car is a piece of crap. Why don't you just junk it and save yourself the headache.

> MICHAEL
> And what am I supposed to drive to work?

> CHARLIE
> Buy a new car. You're working two jobs now, right?

> MICHAEL
> Do I look like I got money for a new car?

CHARLIE

So then ask your old man for a loan. He must have some
money.

MICHAEL

What do I look like to you? I'm not about to ask my parents for
money.

CHARLIE

What's the big deal? They're your parents, they're supposed to
give you money.

MICHAEL

Yeah, well maybe if I still lived at home, they'd make my bed
too. You know, that's just not my style.

CHARLIE slams down the hood and they walk to the office.

CHARLIE

So by the way, I was at the diner the other day and I saw
Claudia. But I noticed she didn't have a ring on her finger.
What's up with that?

MICHAEL

That's because she doesn't have one. I figured I'll buy the ring
after I buy the new car.

CHARLIE

You guys are engaged though, right?

MICHAEL

Yeah, we are. But like I told you before, until we decide exactly
on a date we're not gonna make it official. Neither one of us is
going anywhere.

CHARLIE

I gotta tell you, I'm jealous of you, you know, because I'm
starting to think that's what I'd really like to do. Find a girl and
settle down.

MICHAEL

Yeah, you should.

CHARLIE

Yeah, the only problem is, it seems that all the girls I used to know around here are already spoken for.

MICHAEL

Yeah. And try not to forget that.

CHARLIE

Don't worry. I'm not about to.

MICHAEL

So you gonna help me out, or what?

CHARLIE

Yeah, of course, you cheap bastard, I'll help you out.

MICHAEL

Good. So when can you come and take a look at it? It died outside the house.

CHARLIE

I'm off on Saturday, if that's good for you?

MICHAEL

No. I gotta work on Saturday, how's Sunday?

CHARLIE

Yeah whatever. Sunday's fine. I'll come by on Sunday.

CHARLIE gives MICHAEL a slap on the shoulder.

◘EXT: CHARLIE'S CAR. DAY

Cloudy ugly day. CHARLIE speeds through town.

◘EXT: CLAUDIA AND MICHAEL'S HOUSE. DAY

CHARLIE pulls up in the truck behind MICHAEL'S car and gets out. CHARLIE knocks on the screen door. No answer. He sees the door is open and steps inside.

◘INT: CLAUDIA AND MICHAEL'S STAIRWELL. DAY

> CHARLIE
> Hello?

No answer.

CHARLIE climbs the stairs and knocks on the door at the head of the stairs. We hear a radio playing. CHARLIE opens the door and steps in.

◘INT: CLAUDIA AND MICHAEL'S KITCHEN. DAY

CHARLIE enters.

> CHARLIE
> Yo, Michael, Claudia. Anybody home?

CHARLIE picks up a picture of MIKE and CLAUDIA. He smirks and puts it down.

◘INT: CLAUDIA AND MICHAEL'S BATHROOM. DAY

CLAUDIA steps out of the bathroom getting ready for work. She is wearing just a robe and her hair is wet. She hears CHARLIE and steps out into her bedroom.

◘INT: CLAUDIA AND MICHAEL'S KITCHEN. DAY

CLAUDIA heads toward the kitchen and spots CHARLIE going through their fridge. She is pissed.

> CLAUDIA
> You want to tell me what the hell you are doing in here?

> CHARLIE
> Oh, hey Claudia. What's up?

> CLAUDIA
> Don't "What's up" me. What are you doing here?

CHARLIE

Oh, thanks. Yeah, it's good to see you too.

CLAUDIA

I'm not joking here, Charlie. What are you doing in my
house?

CHARLIE

I came by to see Michael. I knocked on the door, but nobody
answered.

CLAUDIA

So you just let yourself in and started helping yourself to our
beer?

CHARLIE

Yeah. So is he around?

CLAUDIA

No, he's at work. Why? What do you want him for?

CHARLIE

I'm here to fix the car.

CLAUDIA

He told me you were supposed to come by tomorrow.

CHARLIE

Yeah, but I got to work tomorrow, so I figured I'd do it today.

CLAUDIA

You just don't give up, do you? You knew he wasn't gonna be
home today, right?

CHARLIE
(smiling)

No, I mean, he may have mentioned it but—

CLAUDIA

Well, then, why don't you just come back tomorrow like you
said you were going to?

CHARLIE

Because I got to cover for The Foot tomorrow, so if Michael wants his car fixed for Monday morning I can only do it now.

CLAUDIA

So, is this gonna be the routine now? You're gonna hassle me every chance you get?

CHARLIE

Hassle you? I come over here on my day off to fix your boyfriend's car—for free, no less—and you accuse me of hassling you? You think I got nothing better to do than to come over here when I know Michael's not home and see if I can sweet-talk you for a few hours? Come on. I'm not that kind of guy.

CLAUDIA can't help but smile. CHARLIE steps closer to her in the small kitchen.

CLAUDIA

You're not gonna give up with this, are you?

CHARLIE

No, I'm not.

CHARLIE moves closer.

CHARLIE

Look, I asked you what I did the other day because . . . and don't laugh now but . . . I think I might, you know . . . Well, I was thinking a lot about you out there and thinking about how I fucked up and how much . . . I missed you. And that's why I came home. And that's why I'm hassling you.

CHARLIE moves in closer. CLAUDIA turns away from him and goes to the sink. Her back is to him. CHARLIE sneaks up behind her and puts his arms around her.

CLAUDIA

Please don't.

CHARLIE
You didn't miss me at all?

CLAUDIA
Yeah, I missed you.

CHARLIE
So what do you say?

CHARLIE starts to kiss her neck, but she stops him and turns around into him. He's still holding her. He goes to kiss her but she pushes him away.

CLAUDIA
No way, Charlie. No way am I going through that again.

They stand there looking at each other, both not sure who's going to make the next move.

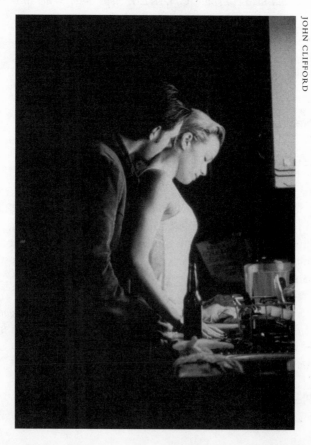

JOHN CLIFFORD

Just then, heard offscreen . . .

> TERESA
> *(OS)*
>
> Claudia, are you home?

> CLAUDIA
>
> Umm, yeah Teresa, I'm up here.

> CHARLIE
>
> Ahh, fuck.

CLAUDIA turns back to the sink and throws some water on her face and quickly dries it off. TERESA enters.

> TERESA
> *(suspiciously)*
>
> Hey, Claudia. Hello, Charlie.

> CHARLIE
>
> Hey, Teresa, how you been?

> TERESA
>
> I been fine. What about you, you keeping outta trouble?

> CHARLIE
>
> Yeah, but I've been trying to convince your friend here to change all that.

> CLAUDIA
>
> He's here to fix Michael's car.

TERESA suspects something is up. She looks at CLAUDIA and then CHARLIE.

> CHARLIE
>
> Yeah, I'm here to fix the car. I'm gonna grab that beer and get started down there then.

> CLAUDIA
>
> Help yourself.

CHARLIE opens the fridge and grabs one. He offers one to the girls and CLAUDIA accepts. CHARLIE then exits. CLAUDIA cracks open her beer and sits down.

TERESA

So?

CLAUDIA

So what?

TERESA

Don't pull that shit with me. What was going on?

CLAUDIA

Nothing was going on. He came up here for a beer.

TERESA

Claudia, please. It's obvious something was going on.

CLAUDIA

I'm telling you, Teresa, we were just talking, that's it.

TERESA

If I was you, I wouldn't even give him that much.

CLAUDIA

Well, you're not me, are you?

◘ INT: CLAUDIA'S MOM'S HOUSE. EVENING

CLAUDIA walks out of the kitchen with a bottle of wine and enters the dining room. MICHAEL and MOM are seated at the small table, having just finished dinner.

CLAUDIA

Come on, Kelly, where are you?

KELLY
(OS)

Hold your horses. I'm coming.

                              MOM

Did she show you what she's going to wear? She looks like a
goddamn hooker.

                            CLAUDIA

Mom, don't start with her tonight.

                             KELLY
                             (OS)

Here I come.

*KELLY appears at the top of the stairs and walks down. This is the best we've
seen her. Everyone just stares.*

                             KELLY

So? What do you think?

                            CLAUDIA

Oh, my God?

                             KELLY

What?

                            CLAUDIA

You look beautiful.

                            MICHAEL

Kelly, you really do. You look great.

                             KELLY
                      (pointing to her cleavage)
Really? You don't think it's too much?

                            MICHAEL

No. If you got it, flaunt it.

                             KELLY

I figured what the hell, a date with Marty the fishmonger has
got to be better than sitting home alone with Mom another
night. What do you think, Mom?

MOM

I think you look like a floozie, but you've been dressing like that since you were thirteen. And you didn't care what I thought then either.

KELLY
(goofing on Mom)
Oh, don't say that, Mom. I care what you think.

KELLY leans over her MOM and gives her a kiss on the cheek. MOM grabs KELLY'S face and laughs.

MOM

Get outta here.

CLAUDIA

So where you guys going?

KELLY

Marino's.

MICHAEL

Wow, Marino's. That's expensive. This guy must make some decent money.

KELLY

Hey, he's got his own shop.

Just then we hear a car horn.

KELLY

That's him.

MOM

Apparently he doesn't have manners, though, does he? Doesn't even come to the front door to say hello. What, are you embarrassed by your family?

KELLY
(heading to the door)
No, he's just afraid of you, Mom. He's heard the stories.

◘INT: CLAUDIA'S MOM'S FRONT HALLWAY. EVENING

CLAUDIA follows KELLY as she goes to the front door, and helps her on with her coat.

> KELLY
>
> What do you think?

> CLAUDIA
>
> I think you're going to have a great time.

> KELLY
>
> Can you believe, I'm actually nervous? Do I look okay?

> CLAUDIA
>
> Don't worry. You look great. Now go have a good time.

> KELLY
>
> Thanks. I love you.

CLAUDIA smiles. The girls kiss and hug. KELLY exits.

◘EXT: CLAUDIA'S MOM'S HOUSE. DUSK

CLAUDIA watches from the door as MARTY, 43, a short guy, opens up the passenger door of his Monte Carlo for KELLY. They take off. CLAUDIA closes the door.

◘EXT: THE LOST BEACH PUB. NIGHT

A bouncer tosses a guy out on his ass.

◘INT: THE LOST BEACH PUB. NIGHT

It's Friday night, and the bar is packed. Assorted white boys and girls sit at the bar. Their heads bob to some seventies guitar rock on the jukebox.

◼INT: THE LOST BEACH PUB BATHROOM. NIGHT

CLAUDIA is standing at the mirror in the ladies' room putting on her lipstick. She stops and looks at herself. ALICE walks into the bathroom and starts to do her makeup next to her.

> ALICE
>
> Hey, Claudia.

> CLAUDIA
>
> Hey, Alice.

> ALICE
>
> So, I heard Charlie's been doing lunch over at the diner. What's up with that?

> CLAUDIA
>
> Where'd you hear that?

> ALICE
>
> People talk.

> CLAUDIA
>
> Well, I wouldn't listen to them.

> ALICE
>
> Whatever you say.

CLAUDIA exits.

◼INT: THE LOST BEACH PUB. NIGHT

CLAUDIA walks out into the crowded and noisy bar.

Cut to:

We will crosscut between ongoing conversations at the bar. The two UPS guys from the diner, now out of uniform, stand against the wall.

> BNO
>
> Come on, it's just fifty. I'll pay you back next week.

SCO

What are you kidding me? I'm into my bookie for almost two hundred from last weekend and I'm gonna lend you fifty that I'll never see? Might's never.

Cut to:

MELISSA and CLAUDIA sit in a booth. MELISSA is holding the sonogram.

MELISSA

Can you see it?

CLAUDIA

No.

MELISSA

No, look at it this way.

She turns the picture upside down.

CLAUDIA

Oh, yeah. Look at that. It's a little one, huh?

MELISSA

Yeah, he takes after his father.

Cut to:

Three girls at the bar.

JENNIFER

Oh, did you see her? She's disgusting. She's covered in tattoos and she's ten years older than him. I don't know what he's thinking, marrying her.

SHARI

I know what he's thinking. Her father gave him a job down at the yard. God knows the drunken fool couldn't get one on his own.

LEAH

That has nothing to do with it. He got her pregnant is what happened. And her father threatened to cut his balls off if he didn't marry her.

Cut to:

GOLDIE and MICHAEL stand at the corner of the bar.

MICHAEL

So he came over to fix the car on Saturday when I told him to come by on Sunday, 'cause he knew I wasn't gonna be around that day. I told you the guy's a fucking dog.

GOLDIE

Did he fix the car?

MICHAEL

Yeah, but that's not the point. I know he's up to something. I swear, if he tries anything with her, I'll kill him.

GOLDIE

Michael, come on, he told you himself he wouldn't do anything.

MICHAEL

Oh. Well, that makes me feel much better. You act like this guy has actually kept his word once or twice.

Cut to:

Two guys standing against the wall.

GUY

So what happened to you out in Long Beach?

GUY 2

They misunderstood what I said. So it couldn't happen out there.

GUY

Oh, that sucks. That would have been cool to do this out there.

Cut to:

TERESA and TONY the pizza guy are at the pinball machine.

TERESA
Oh, that's so sad. When did you guys break up?

TONY
About two weeks ago.

TERESA
So you're not seeing anybody else now, are you?

TONY
No, not yet.

TERESA
Well, that's good. You should take your time with that.
You wouldn't want to rush right into something. Would
you?

Cut to:

A couple sitting at the bar.

BOB
Come on, baby. Let me just touch them.

MAGGIE
Get the hell out of here, you friggin' pervert.

BOB
Come on, just one little touch.

MAGGIE gets up from the bar.

Cut to:

CLAUDIA and MELISSA at the booth. TERESA runs over.

TERESA
Tony from the pizza place is here.

CLAUDIA

So?

TERESA

So he broke up with his girlfriend. And I'm talking to him, and I'm thinking maybe . . .

CLAUDIA

Yeah?

TERESA
(beat)
Do you guys have any rubbers on you? Just in case.

Cut to:

JENNIFER, SHARI, and LEAH are sitting at the booth.

JENNIFER

You hear who moved in on State Street?

SHARI

Yeah, I know. Can you believe the O'Haras sold their house to them? I saw them moving in the other day.

LEAH

That whole part of the neighborhood's captured territory now. You can't even drink at Smitty's anymore. It's a fucking shame.

SHARI

I'm telling you. I give my mother a week before she's got her house up for sale.

Cut to:

GOLDIE and MICHAEL belly up to the bar at the far corner.

MICHAEL

So explain to me why he had to go into the house?

GOLDIE

He wanted a beer.

MICHAEL
So he had to come into the house?

GOLDIE
Mike, the guy's fixing your car for free, I'd say it's not out of bounds for him to ask for a beer.

MICHAEL
Tell me the truth, you think he tried anything?

GOLDIE
Don't you think she would've told you?

MICHAEL
I don't know.
(beat)
Yeah, she would, wouldn't she?

GOLDIE
Yeah.

MICHAEL
(looking up)
And look what just walked in.

◼INT: THE LOST BEACH PUB. NIGHT

A new song starts and all other audio is out. Then in slo-mo CHARLIE steps in through the front door with ANNIE, 18, a very hot young girl. They head through the bar, arm in arm.

At the booth, MELISSA taps CLAUDIA'S arm and she turns around to see them.

Against the wall, TERESA and TONY watch.

At the bar, GOLDIE and MICHAEL watch as he heads their way. Just as CHARLIE and ANNIE approach GOLDIE and MICHAEL, the sound pops back in and we are back in regular time.

CHARLIE

There they are. Hey, fellas, how you doing?

GOLDIE

Hey, Charlie, what's doing?

CHARLIE

Guys, I want you to meet . . . Annie. Annie, I want you to meet
Goldie and Michael. These two mutts here are my oldest friends
in the world.

MICHAEL

Yeah, and maybe his only friends too.

CHARLIE

It's true. I've known these guys since I was even younger than
you. So you gotta be nice to them.

GOLDIE

Hey, Annie. It's very nice to meet you.

CHARLIE

So, Michael, how's the car running? I don't get a thank-you call?

MICHAEL

Good. But what happened to coming over on Sunday?

CHARLIE

Didn't Claudia tell you? I had to cover for The Foot on Sunday,
so I could only do it on Saturday.

MICHAEL

Do me a favor. Next time that happens, call me ahead of time,
okay?

CHARLIE

Yeah, sure, whatever.

GOLDIE

So what's up, Charlie, are we on for that poker game next
week?

CHARLIE

Yeah, you kidding me? And I'm gonna take all your friggin' money. What about you Mikey? Are you gonna play?

MICHAEL

Yeah, I'll be there.

ANNIE

Hey, I'll be right back. I'm just gonna go to the bathroom, okay?

CHARLIE

Yeah. Just don't leave without me, all right, sweetheart?

He gives her a kiss and she goes. CLAUDIA watches.

GOLDIE

So you guys need a drink or what?

MICHAEL

No. I'm good.

CHARLIE turns to the bartender.

GOLDIE

Billy, three shots of Jack down here.
          (turning back around)
So, where did you find her?

CHARLIE

Yeah, I know. Is she fuckin' hot or what?

MICHAEL

I hope you're not thinking about taking that girl home?

CHARLIE

Only if I'm fucking lucky tonight.

MICHAEL

Charlie, she's just a little kid. You can't do that.

CHARLIE

What are you talking about? I can do whatever I want. She told me she's a freshman in college or somethin'.

MICHAEL

That's fucked up, man. Look, I'm outta here.

MICHAEL just shakes his head and walks away.

CHARLIE

All of a sudden he's a fucking saint?

GOLDIE

Don't worry about it. Let's do these shots. And if I was you . . .

MICHAEL gets CLAUDIA from the booth and they head toward the door. The boys turn and grab their shots. CHARLIE puts his glass down and looks toward the door. CLAUDIA and MICHAEL are heading out. She turns back and looks at him. CHARLIE drops his eyes and does the other shot.

◘ EXT: THE LOST BEACH PUB. NIGHT

CLAUDIA and MICHAEL walk out of the bar.

MICHAEL

I'm sorry. I really just can't stand to be near that guy.

MICHAEL puts on his jacket. CLAUDIA sighs. She's heard this kind of shit all her life.

MICHAEL

Come on.

MICHAEL puts his arm around CLAUDIA, and they head off down the street.

◘ INT: CHARLIE'S CAR. NIGHT

CHARLIE and ANNIE sit in the front seat making out. She stops him.

ANNIE

Wait a second.

CHARLIE

What's wrong?

ANNIE

We shouldn't be doing this out here. Somebody might
see us.

CHARLIE

Well, then, let's go inside.

ANNIE

I told you we can't. My parents are home.

CHARLIE

You got any money on you or a credit card?

ANNIE

Yeah.

CHARLIE

So then let's go to a motel room.

ANNIE

I don't . . . I don't . . . know. . . .

CHARLIE

What? Is something wrong?

ANNIE

No. I'm just not ready to do this right now, that's all.

CHARLIE

What are you scared of? Do I look like I'm gonna hurt you or
something? Look at me. I'm a fucking pussycat over here.

ANNIE

No. But look, it's already almost five in the morning. My parents
are gonna be up soon.

CHARLIE
So what are you saying? You want to go home?

ANNIE
Look, I'm gonna be home again in like a month or so for spring break. Maybe we should just wait till then?

CHARLIE
Yeah, sure. I'll be waiting by the fucking phone.

CHARLIE turns and looks out the front window. ANNIE reaches over and kisses him. She then jumps out of the car and runs up the long walk to her house. CHARLIE takes off.

◘EXT: QUIET STREET. DAWN

CHARLIE drives, quiet and sullen. He then abruptly turns off the road.

◘EXT: BEACH. DAWN

Charlie's car shoots out onto the beach and starts doing doughnuts, then stops and sits. CHARLIE sits and then slams the steering wheel. The car slowly drives off the beach.

JOHN CLIFFORD

◻INT: PIZZA PLACE. DAY

TONY, the big Italian kid from the bar, is behind the counter. He slices up a pie and throws CLAUDIA a few slices.

> ### TONY
> What you want with that, a Coke, Sprite or—?

> ### CLAUDIA
> Coke's good. Two Cokes.

> ### TONY
> Two Cokes coming up. Hey, by the way, how's Mikey doing?
> Everything's all right with you guys?

> ### CLAUDIA
> Yeah, everything's fine. Why?

> ### TONY
> No reason. Just want to make sure, you know. Because I like
> Michael, he's a good guy.

> ### CLAUDIA
> Thanks, Anthony. Things are fine, though. I'm gonna go sit
> down now.

> ### TONY
> All right. I'll be here if you need me.

CLAUDIA walks to the back and sits down at a table where TERESA is waiting.

> ### TERESA
> What do you think of him?

> ### CLAUDIA
> Who? Anthony?

> ### TERESA
> Yeah, you think he's cute, at all?

CLAUDIA

Not really my type.

TERESA

I always thought he was kind of sexy in high school.

CLAUDIA

So ask him out.

TERESA

I tried asking him out the other night at the bar, but he didn't get the hint. Besides, I think he got back with his girlfriend. I wouldn't feel right about that.

CLAUDIA

Yeah, right. Well just say that you're sitting home alone one night. . . .

TERESA

What do you mean, one night? Try every night.

CLAUDIA

Okay. So you're home alone, again. And you decide to have some pizza delivered. And our man Anthony shows up at the door. Would you invite him in?

TERESA

Would I invite him in? Please, in a heartbeat.

CLAUDIA

Okay. So now that you got him in, what do you do?

TERESA

Do I think he's into me?

CLAUDIA

Oh, yeah, you can tell. He wants you.

TERESA

Okay. So I make a move.

CLAUDIA

And?

TERESA

And what? You mean would I have sex with him?

CLAUDIA

Yeah.

TERESA

Well, if you're gonna do it, you might as well do it right.
Right?

CLAUDIA

What about the girlfriend?

TERESA
(laughing)
Fuck her. If he's coming after me, she's obviously not treating
him right.

They laugh.

TERESA

Now let me ask you a question. Is that what happened when
Charlie came over to fix the car?

CLAUDIA
(hesitating)
I told you we were just talking.
(beat)

TERESA says nothing, but that's what she expected.

◾ EXT: BUGSY'S GAS STATION. DAY

*THE FOOT finishes filling the tank, collects the cash, and heads back into the
gas station, dragging his club foot.*

◘INT: BUGSY'S GAS STATION. DAY

THE FOOT steps in from the rain and throws off his slicker. CHARLIE stands there putting on his coat.

> CHARLIE
> Tell me something, Foot. What the hell are you still doing working here pumping gas? A guy your age.

> FOOT
> Same thing you're doing, making the rent.

> CHARLIE
> Hey, don't go comparing my life to your life, okay, pal? I ain't here to make the friggin' rent.

CHARLIE then steps into the garage where BUGSY is working under a car.

> CHARLIE
> Hey, Bugs, I'm gonna grab some lunch, okay?

> BUGSY
> Yeah, just don't take all fucking day, Charlie.

CHARLIE nods and steps back into the office with THE FOOT.

> CHARLIE
> Making the fucking rent, my ass. Listen, I'm going to go get me some lunch. You want anything?

THE FOOT holds up a brown bag. CHARLIE shakes his head and heads out.

◘INT: LAUNDROMAT. DAY

CLAUDIA loads a machine as a radio plays.

◘EXT: LAUNDROMAT. DAY

CHARLIE'S truck drives past CLAUDIA'S parked car. He quickly does a U-turn and parks behind it. CHARLIE grabs a bag off the passenger seat.

◻INT: LAUNDROMAT. DAY

CLAUDIA looks up as CHARLIE enters. She shakes her head and smiles.

> ### CHARLIE
> What are you smiling at?

> ### CLAUDIA
> You just come back from the junior high school?

> ### CHARLIE
> Hey. She was in college. Besides, I just drove her home.

> ### CLAUDIA
> Yeah, I'm sure you did.

> ### CHARLIE
> I brought you some lunch. You want a half a meatball
> hero?

> ### CLAUDIA
> No, thanks.

> ### CHARLIE
> How about a beer, then? I got some beers.

> ### CLAUDIA
> A beer I'll take.

> ### CHARLIE
> Yeah, I figured as much.

CHARLIE pulls out two cans of beer and pops them open. She is smiling at him again.

> ### CHARLIE
> I'm telling you the truth, nothing happened. I just drove her
> home, a little kiss, and that was it. What? Are you jealous or
> something?

> ### CLAUDIA
> Why would I be jealous?

CHARLIE

No reason. I'm just saying if you are jealous, it's okay. I can understand. I'm sure it was weird for you to see me with another woman. Especially a fine young little thing like that.

CLAUDIA

If I thought there was a chance she might be out of the tenth grade, then maybe I might be jealous.

CHARLIE

I told you, she was in college.

CLAUDIA

I hope so for your sake.

CHARLIE *goes over to the radio and raises the volume.*

CHARLIE

Oh, I know this song. You like this song, don't you?

CLAUDIA

You know I like all his stuff.

CHARLIE

You want to dance?

CLAUDIA

What? Here?

CHARLIE

Yeah, come on. A little slow dance.

CLAUDIA

What are you talking about? You don't know how to dance.

CHARLIE

What? It's a slow dance. Any retard knows how to do a little slow dance. Besides, you don't remember our prom? We did some dancing that night, didn't we?

CLAUDIA

I don't think so.

CHARLIE playfully grabs her arms and tries to sway her.

CHARLIE

Come on, one dance.

CLAUDIA

I'm sorry. I can't.

They stand there, looking at each other.

CHARLIE

You hate me, don't you?

CLAUDIA

No, I'm just not dancing with you.

CHARLIE

All right. I guess I should probably be getting back to work now anyhow, huh?

CLAUDIA shrugs, suggesting that he should. CHARLIE grabs his bag and heads out. He stops at the door.

CHARLIE

All right, I'll see you around. Enjoy the beer.

He stops at the door.

CHARLIE

Hey.

CLAUDIA

What?

CHARLIE
(with a smile)
I told you you'd be cleaning his dirty underwear.

CLAUDIA smirks and gives him the finger. He smiles and turns and exits.

◘EXT: BALL FIELD. DAY

CLAUDIA and MICHAEL cut across a ball field on the way to the bar.

MICHAEL

You okay?

CLAUDIA

Yeah.

MICHAEL

You sure?

CLAUDIA

I said I'm fine.

MICHAEL

What? You don't want to go to the bar to watch the game, do you?

CLAUDIA

No, forget it, it's fine.

MICHAEL

Look, if you don't want to go to the bar, I understand. What do you say we go over to my mother's house for dinner tonight instead and have a nice big meal. Everybody's gonna be there. It'll be good.

CLAUDIA
(getting up)
Couldn't we go into the city and go to a nice restaurant instead?

MICHAEL

I just finished telling you that we can barely afford our bills, and you want to go into the city to a restaurant. Why would we go all the way into the city?

CLAUDIA

Because we haven't left this town to do anything in over a year. It would be nice to see something other than the same people and the same streets. Besides, every time we go over to your mother's, you and your brothers sit in the living room and watch football, and your mother and sister trap me in the kitchen and ask me when are we going to get married.

MICHAEL

No, they don't.

CLAUDIA

Yes, they do. Every time.

MICHAEL

And what do you say to them?

CLAUDIA

The same thing I always say to you.

MICHAEL

Yeah. Which is bullshit.

CLAUDIA

Please don't start with that tonight, Michael.

MICHAEL

Don't start with that? Listen, Claudia, I'm not gonna wait till
I'm an old man to get married, you know. I'm ready.

CLAUDIA

I know you're ready. In fact, everybody we know, knows how
ready you are.

MICHAEL

Then what the hell are we waiting for? I mean, we've been
together forever, what more do you want?

CLAUDIA

I don't know what I want. That's what I've been trying to tell
you. But you don't want to hear that.

MICHAEL

Because it doesn't make any sense. You're almost thirty years old;
you're not getting any younger. When do you think you're
going to want to do this?

CLAUDIA

I just don't want to rush into it, Michael.

MICHAEL

What am I doing here? Am I just wasting my time here? 'Cause
if I am, tell me and I'll get on with my life.

CLAUDIA

Why do you insist on hounding me about this?

MICHAEL

What are you talking about, hounding? I'm not fucking
hounding you about anything. I love you and I want to marry
you. That would be my dream come true. Why do you see that
as me hounding you?

CLAUDIA
(yelling)

Because we have this same conversation every week. No, I don't
want to have dinner at your mother's, and no, I'm just not ready
to get married yet. Okay. That's it.

MICHAEL

Why the fuck not?

CLAUDIA

Because I'm not ready to become a goddamn housewife, that's
why.

MICHAEL

Who said you had to be a housewife?

CLAUDIA
(starting to cry)
What else would I be? Tell me what else I would be if we got
married right now? What the hell would I do with the rest of
my life?

MICHAEL
(stammering)
I don't know.

CLAUDIA
(in tears)
That's exactly my point. Neither do I.

◼EXT: MAIN STREET. DAY

*CLAUDIA and KELLY walk down Main Street. KELLY pushes the baby
carriage.*

KELLY

What's with the sour puss today?

CLAUDIA

Nothing.

KELLY

Don't give me that, Claudia. You been acting pissy all
morning.

CLAUDIA

I don't know. Do you ever feel like your life is just a series of,
like, regrets and mistakes?

KELLY

No. I mean, sure, there are some things I wish I hadn't done, but
I've always made my own choices. So if it's a good choice or bad
choice, I take responsibility. And that's all there is to it;
sometimes those choices feel good and sometimes they hurt.
You know?

CLAUDIA

Yeah. But what if you have the feeling that, no matter what
choice you make, you're just gonna be hurting in the end.

KELLY

Oh, then, then you're fucked.

CLAUDIA

Oh, thanks a lot. That's real helpful. So what's going on with
Marty? How was the date?

KELLY

It was good.

CLAUDIA

Really? So you like this guy?

KELLY

He's a very nice guy.

CLAUDIA

So is this a real love affair or something?

KELLY

Well, he's hardly my dream come true. . . .

CLAUDIA

Whose does?

KELLY smiles.

KELLY

But yeah, I think this might actually work. And he loves the
baby. So, I'm thinking I'm gonna stick with him for a while.

CLAUDIA

Good.

◘ EXT: DINER. NIGHT

The lights inside the diner go off. Then the neon lights outside are turned off. CLAUDIA and the OLDER WAITRESS step outside and say their good-byes. CLAUDIA locks up.

◘ EXT: CLAUDIA'S MOM'S HOUSE. MORNING

KELLY walks up the front stoop with her baby.

◘ INT: CLAUDIA'S MOM'S HOUSE. DAY

KELLY enters the house with her baby in her arms. She calls for her mother. No answer. KELLY then walks down the hall and stops at her mother's bedroom door.

KELLY

Oh, my god.

KELLY'S knees buckle and she grabs the door. MOM lies on the floor, not moving.

◘ EXT: CLAUDIA'S MOM'S HOUSE. DAY

MICHAEL and CLAUDIA pull up in a hurry in Claudia's car. KELLY is standing outside. They get out of the car.

CLAUDIA

What happened? Is she okay?

KELLY

Yeah, thank god. The doctor came by and said there's nothing wrong with her, she just collapsed. Now she's upstairs sleeping, finally.

CLAUDIA

Well, what happened?

KELLY
(very upset)

Dad called. He's such a piece of shit. You know why he called?
He's in love and he's found himself. Oh, yeah, and to tell her she
could have the fucking house. He's livin' down in Vegas now and
he said we won't be hearing from him anymore and doesn't
want us to call him either. I told you he never gave a shit about
us. I swear I hope he fucking dies tomorrow.
(starting to break down)
And you know when he called, she just sat there on the phone
listening to him, not saying nothing. And then she hung up real
calm, told me what he said, and went to bed. And this morning
when I left for Mass she was still asleep. So I figured she'd be fine.
And then I come home to find her sprawled out on the floor.

*KELLY starts to cry. CLAUDIA goes over and hugs her. KELLY cries on her
shoulder.*

◘ INT: CLAUDIA'S MOM'S LIVING ROOM. SAME DAY

MICHAEL, MARTY, and KELLY sit in silence. KELLY'S baby cries.

◘ INT: CLAUDIA'S MOM'S BEDROOM. DAY

*CLAUDIA stands at the doorway and looks down at her mother. MOM opens
her eyes and gives a little smile and motions for CLAUDIA to come over.
CLAUDIA walks over and grabs her hand.*

MOM
(speaks softly)

Hey, baby.

CLAUDIA

How you doing?

MOM

Oh, I'm just fine.

MOM reaches out and touches Claudia's face. CLAUDIA is starting to cry.

MOM

You always were my beautiful baby. Hey, don't you cry about a thing. I told you he's done this before. Just you wait, he's gonna be home soon and I don't want him to see you crying, okay, okay?

CLAUDIA

Yeah. Okay.

MOM

Good girl. Now I'm gonna take a little nap, but you be sure to wake me when he gets here.

She turns over and closes her eyes.

◻EXT: CLAUDIA AND MICHAEL'S STOOP. DUSK

CLAUDIA sits on the stoop. MICHAEL exits and sits next to her.

CLAUDIA

It's weird, you know. Something like this happens, and you realize that all that other stuff that you think is so important doesn't really matter so much.

JOHN CLIFFORD

MICHAEL

You're wrong. If all the little stuff didn't matter, your mother wouldn't be hurting the way she is.

CLAUDIA turns and looks at him. He's right.

MICHAEL

Don't worry, babe, she's gonna be all right.

CLAUDIA forces a smile.

MICHAEL

You know, what do you say we make that road trip into the city next weekend? We'll go get some dinner or something.

CLAUDIA
(not really interested)
Yeah. That would be nice.

CLAUDIA stands up.

CLAUDIA

I think I'm gonna take a walk.

MICHAEL

You want any company?

CLAUDIA

No. I need to be alone for a little bit.

MICHAEL watches her walk away.

◘EXT: BEACH. EVENING

CLAUDIA walks onto the boardwalk and crosses to the railing. She stares out at the waves.

◘INT: DINER. DAY

CLAUDIA is at work. She looks miserable. She pours the coffee and serves the eggs.

◘EXT: CLAUDIA AND MICHAEL'S HOUSE. NIGHT

CLAUDIA pulls her car up into the driveway and parks. She carries herself into the house. She passes by the garbage cans.

◘INT: CLAUDIA AND MICHAEL'S LIVING ROOM AND KITCHEN. DUSK

CLAUDIA walks into the living room and hits the answering machine. She walks back into the kitchen and sits down at the table.

> MACHINE (TERESA)
> Hey, Claudia, it's Teresa. Give me a call. I'm thinking about having some pizza delivered. You've got to come up with a plan for me. 'Bye.

> MACHINE (GOLDIE)
> Hey, guys, it's Goldie and Missy. We're gonna be down at the bar tonight if you want to have a drink. See you later.

> MACHINE (MICHAEL)
> Hey, babe, it's me. Listen, I'm gonna do a double shift tonight so I won't be home till morning. I'll call back later. I got you some flowers. I hope you like them. Love you.

CLAUDIA gets up and grabs the phone. She starts to dial a number and then stops. She hangs up and grabs a beer.

◘INT: CLAUDIA AND MICHAEL'S LIVING ROOM. NIGHT

CLAUDIA walks into the living room and clicks on the TV. She falls into the couch.

◘INT: CLAUDIA AND MICHAEL'S BEDROOM. NIGHT

CLAUDIA and MICHAEL lie in bed. MICHAEL is asleep. CLAUDIA looks at the ceiling.

◘INT: DINER. DAY

The diner is quiet. CLAUDIA sits at the counter doing her nails. She then looks down at the OLDER WAITRESS, who is sitting, filing her nails laughing with some guy. CLAUDIA gets up and goes to the pay phone and dials.

CLAUDIA
Can I speak with Charlie please?

◘INT: BUGSY'S GAS STATION. DAY

Crosscut:

CHARLIE on the phone.

CHARLIE
Yeah, who's this?

CLAUDIA
It's me, Claudia.

CHARLIE
Hey. How you been?

CLAUDIA

Okay. What about you?

CHARLIE

Good. I been thinking a lot about you.

An uncomfortable silence.

CHARLIE

You still there?

CLAUDIA

Yeah.

(beat)

How long are you going to be there today?

CHARLIE

I'm stuck here all night. Why?

CLAUDIA

Well, I get off in about an hour. You mind if I stop by to say hello?

CHARLIE

Are you kidding me? No, come on over.

CLAUDIA

You're not gonna have the cheerleading squad with you, are you?

CHARLIE

Don't be a wiseass.

CLAUDIA

(laughs)

I'll see you in a little bit.

CLAUDIA hangs up the phone.

◘EXT: BUGSY'S GAS STATION. DAY

CLAUDIA pulls up into the gas station. CHARLIE sees her and casually walks up to her car, opens the passenger-side door, climbs in, and gives her a kiss on the cheek. She lets him get away with it.

CHARLIE
Where to?

CLAUDIA
What do you mean, where to?

CHARLIE
I took the rest of the day off. So let's go someplace.

She smiles and hits the gas. They speed out of the gas station.

◘EXT: BEACH CLUB. DAY

A short three-shot montage of beach club: the empty rows and rows of boarded-up cabanas.

◘EXT: BEACH CLUB. DAY

CLAUDIA and CHARLIE walk through the quiet run-down club.

JOHN CLIFFORD

CHARLIE

So Teresa seems like she still hates me, huh?

CLAUDIA

Yeah.

CHARLIE

And your sister?

CLAUDIA

Of course.

CHARLIE

I'm sure Michael must, too.

CLAUDIA

What do you think?

CHARLIE

And what about you?

CLAUDIA

Out of all of them I'm the one who should hate you, but . . .

CHARLIE

But you can't.

CLAUDIA
(laughing)
No, as hard as I try I can't.

CHARLIE

You see, it's always been us two against the rest of them.

CLAUDIA

Do you realize we were in sixth grade the first time we kissed? That's close to twenty years ago. So you've been breaking my

heart on and off for twenty years now. I hope you're proud of
yourself.

> CHARLIE

Jesus, twenty years? That's a little depressing, isn't it?

> CLAUDIA

Forget twenty years; the fact that I still talk to you is
depressing.

They walk on.

◘EXT: CABANA'S END. DAY

*CLAUDIA and CHARLIE enter frame and walk to end of the cabana row
and look out over the water.*

> CLAUDIA

My dad used to take us here all the time when we were kids. He
would take us on the jetty and we'd sit there watching the sun
set. It's funny, when you're a kid you don't really need too much
to make you happy, do you.

> CHARLIE
> *(agreeing)*

Yeah, life would be a lot easier if a fucking lollipop and a pat on
the head could solve all your problems.

CLAUDIA laughs.

> CLAUDIA

Do you think we screwed up somehow? I mean, is this how we
were supposed to end up?

> CHARLIE

Why would you say "end up"? You're talking like your life's
already over.

CLAUDIA

Because I can feel it closing in. There's always something. I mean, look at my father, for one. That's why he left.

CHARLIE

If you feel that way, then why don't you come away with me when I go?

CLAUDIA

Come on, Charlie, you know I can't do that.

CHARLIE

Why not?

CLAUDIA

Because you hurt me pretty good last time and I don't want to get hurt again.

CHARLIE

Hey, I promise you, I'm not gonna hurt you again.
(pause)
Look, I know I screwed up big time back then. Why do you think I was in such a hurry to get outta here? But I'm telling you, it's different now.

CLAUDIA

How is it different?

CHARLIE reaches out and touches her face, bringing it toward his.

CHARLIE

I need you this time.

CLAUDIA

Promise me you're not playing games with my head.

CHARLIE

I promise.

They kiss.

◻INT: CLAUDIA AND MICHAEL'S KITCHEN. MORNING

CLAUDIA is cooking some eggs. MICHAEL enters dressed for work and sits at the kitchen table. CLAUDIA puts a plate down in front of him.

MICHAEL
What's this?

CLAUDIA
Scrambled eggs.

MICHAEL
I can see that. What's the occasion?

CLAUDIA
I don't know. I just thought you might want some eggs, that's all.

She turns back around and starts to clean up.

◼INT: CLAUDIA'S MOM'S BEDROOM. NIGHT

CLAUDIA enters with a drink for MOM, who sits in bed playing cards.

> MOM
>
> Oh, thank you, sweetheart. That'll help.

> CLAUDIA
>
> So, how you feeling, Ma? You want me to fix you something to eat?

> MOM
>
> No, no. I'm feeling all right, I guess. This will do for now. And what are you so chipper about with your poor mother laying here half dead?

> CLAUDIA
>
> Don't talk like that, Ma. And what are you saying? I'm not chipper.

> MOM
>
> Oh yeah? Then what's that smile on your face all about?

> CLAUDIA
>
> I don't know, just stuff.

> MOM
>
> Just stuff? You're not getting yourself into any trouble, are you?

> CLAUDIA
> *(laughing)*
>
> No.

> MOM
>
> Well, if that's the case, why don't you come over here and rub some of that stuff off on your mother, will ya?

CLAUDIA sits next to her mom and lays her head in her lap. MOM strokes her head and looks at the picture of her husband on the wall.

MOM
(almost to herself)
We seem to always fall for the wrong ones in this family, don't
we?

◘INT: CLAUDIA'S MOM'S KITCHEN. NIGHT

CLAUDIA enters the kitchen. KELLY sits there with a cup of coffee.

KELLY
How's she doing up there?

◘INT: CHARLIE'S MOM'S KITCHEN. NIGHT

*CHARLIE, SULLY, 28, GOLDIE, and MICHAEL are sitting around a
table playing cards. MICHAEL picks up two cards.*

MICHAEL
Oh, my. You boys have got some trouble on your hands. Goldie,
I see your fifty cents and I raise you two bucks.

GOLDIE
You sure you can afford that?

MICHAEL
Don't worry about me. What about you, you in or you out?

CHARLIE
Look at Michael. Playing the big spender. Yeah, I'm in, tough
nuts. I see your two bucks and I raise you twenty.

MICHAEL
What are you doing raising me twenty? You know we don't play
for that.

GOLDIE
Yeah, come on, Charlie. You know we don't play for that kind of
money.

CHARLIE

What? He's sitting over there grinning like a big man with a big hand. I want to give him a chance to show us how big he is.

MICHAEL

You're an asshole, you know that?

CHARLIE

You can always fold, tough nuts.

MICHAEL

Goldie, lend me twenty.

GOLDIE

You're into me for almost forty already, Michael.

MICHAEL

Have I ever not paid you back, you cheap bastard? Lend me the money.

GOLDIE tosses MICHAEL a few chips and he puts them on the pile.

MICHAEL

You're a fucking prick, you know that? Okay, scumbag, let's see what you got.

CHARLIE
(showing hand)

Full house.

MICHAEL is pissed. He folds his cards with a slam on the table. He stares at CHARLIE.

MICHAEL

You know you haven't changed a bit. You're still a fucking dirtbag.

CHARLIE

Michael, face it, our entire lives I've been beating your ass. What do you think, that was gonna change all of a sudden?

GOLDIE

Come on Charlie, don't be a dick.

MICHAEL

Don't worry about it. He can't help himself. You know, you little prick, you should have stayed in California.

CHARLIE

Ah, come on. I'm busting your balls. Don't turn into a faggot on us.

GOLDIE

Guys, yo, chill out here. Come on.

SULLY

Yeah, come on, Mikey, lighten up. It's only money.

MICHAEL

Don't push me, Charlie, okay?

CHARLIE

I ain't pushing you anywhere. I'm playing cards. You can't take losing, take a hike.

MICHAEL

Fine. I'm outta here.

GOLDIE

Come on, Mike. Listen, I can lend you more money, don't worry about that.

MICHAEL

No, it's not the money, it's this asshole. And do me a favor, douche bag, keep away from Claudia.

MICHAEL turns and leaves the house.

CHARLIE

Look at that. I fix the guy's car for free, and this is the thanks I get.

GOLDIE

What are you doing?

CHARLIE

What do you mean, what am I doing?

GOLDIE

You're giving him a hard time.

CHARLIE

I'm not giving him a hard time. I'm joking with him.

GOLDIE

So why do you joke with him?

CHARLIE

Hey, Goldie. He's a big boy. He can handle it. Besides, why are you always defending him anyway? You got a hard-on for him or something?

GOLDIE

You're a fucking dog.

CHARLIE

What is that supposed to mean?

GOLDIE

Why don't you tell me.

CHARLIE

What the fuck are you talking about?

GOLDIE

Is something going on with you and Claudia?

CHARLIE

No.

GOLDIE

Well, people are talking, Charlie.

CHARLIE

That's because that's all there is to do here.

GOLDIE shakes his head in disappointment.

GOLDIE

You can't do that to her, Charlie. You can't just show up and
start screwing with her head all over again.

CHARLIE

Who says I'm screwing with her head? Let's just say the only
reason I came back here is because I wanted to see her again,
and I come home to find one of my best friends is shacking up
with her. What am I supposed to do? Just fucking pack up and
take off again?

GOLDIE

Oh, man, give me a break. Next you're gonna tell me that you're
still in love with her after all these years, right?

CHARLIE

Maybe.

GOLDIE

It's just not right, Charlie. What you're doing, it's not right
at all.

CHARLIE

Hey, Goldie, do me a favor and shut the fuck up because we
haven't done anything. We went for a walk and that's it. And as
long as she's still with Michael that's all that's gonna happen.
Okay?

GOLDIE

Should I believe you?

CHARLIE

I don't really give a shit what you do.

GOLDIE looks at CHARLIE and shakes his head in disappointment.

■INT: DINER. MORNING

CLAUDIA stands by the window with her coffee and stares out.

■INT: BUGSY'S GAS STATION'S BATHROOM. DAY

CHARLIE is at the mirror and sink trying to get his hands clean using industrial-strength soap. He changes his shirt, combs his hair, and heads out the door.

■INT: BUGSY'S GAS STATION'S GARAGE. DAY

CHARLIE steps out of the bathroom and into the garage. BUGSY steps out from behind a car and calls for him.

> BUGSY
>
> Hey, Charlie, how much longer you gonna be sticking around for?

> CHARLIE
>
> I don't know really.

> BUGSY
>
> Well, Jimmy here is gonna be leaving at the end of the month, so I'm gonna need a new full-time guy if you're interested.

> CHARLIE
>
> Yeah? Really? Shit. Can I get back to you in a few days?

> BUGSY
>
> Yeah, I'll give you a few days, but just don't jerk me around on this, all right.

> CHARLIE
>
> Yeah, sure.

CHARLIE nods and heads into the office.

INT: BUGSY'S GAS STATION'S OFFICE. DAY

THE FOOT sits at the desk eating his lunch.

> CHARLIE
> Look at you, the fucking happy brown bagger. All right. I'll see you tomorrow.

CHARLIE exits.

INT: DINER. DAY

CLAUDIA scoops some change off a table and throws it in her pocket. She looks up at the clock. Five of four. She quickly clears the table and heads to the kitchen.

INT: DINER BATHROOM. DAY

CLAUDIA enters the bathroom. She pulls off her waitress outfit and throws on jeans and a T-shirt. She fixes her face in the mirror and throws on some perfume, a little under the pits.

INT: DINER KITCHEN. DAY

CLAUDIA walks out into the kitchen and heads for the back door.

> CLAUDIA
> I'll see you guys on Monday.

> OLDER WAITRESS
> And where are you off to, all prettied up?

> CLAUDIA
> Nowhere special.

> OLDER WAITRESS
> Nowhere special?
> *(pause)*

Be careful, Claudia, all right?

The OLDER WAITRESS gives CLAUDIA a knowing smile. CLAUDIA smiles back and heads out through the kitchen.

◻EXT: REAR OF DINER. DAY

CHARLIE'S car is parked outside in the lot. CHARLIE is sitting in the driver's seat. He pops open the passenger-side door. CLAUDIA steps out of the diner and runs down and hops into Charlie's car. They kiss and seem happy.

> CHARLIE
> I don't want to sound like I'm giving you a line but . . . you look really nice.

> CLAUDIA
> Thanks.

> CHARLIE
> So where do you want to go?

> CLAUDIA
> I don't know. Where do you want to go?

> CHARLIE
> You want to go someplace and get a drink?

> CLAUDIA
> Like where?

> CHARLIE
> Let's go down to Asbury again. Nobody's gonna know us there.

◻INT: SMITTY'S. DAY

CHARLIE grabs two beers off the bar and crosses to a booth and sits with CLAUDIA. The bar is almost empty.

CHARLIE

I'm telling you, you'd love it down there. Besides, I got a friend
from California that lives in Gainsville now. We can spend a few
weeks for free at his place until we get set up down there.

CLAUDIA

Why do we want to go to Florida, though? There's nothing but
old people down there.

CHARLIE

You kidding me? It's beautiful down there. And they got nice
beaches too.

CLAUDIA

I don't need any more beaches. What about someplace like
Seattle?

CHARLIE

What about it? It's gray and rainy all the time there too. You
may as well stay here. Besides, I want someplace warm. What
about Las Vegas?

CLAUDIA

No way.

CHARLIE

New Orleans?

CLAUDIA

What about Texas?

CHARLIE

Texas? Yeah, I like Texas. Anywhere in particular? It's a big
state.

CLAUDIA

No. We'll figure it out when we get there.

CHARLIE

All right, Texas it is then. I told you we were meant for one
another.

CHARLIE smiles. CLAUDIA tries to smile back.

CHARLIE

Hey, what's wrong?

CLAUDIA

Do you ever think what our lives would be like now if I had the
baby?

CHARLIE

Yeah, we'd be miserable.

CLAUDIA

Yeah, because things are so great now. Right?

CHARLIE

No. But think about it. You spend your whole life working hard
to feed them, clothe them, put them through school only to
have them tell you to go fuck yourself when they turn sixteen.
No, thanks.

CLAUDIA

Well, considering what I'm about to tell you, I guess that's a
good thing you feel that way. And I haven't told anybody else
this. Not Michael, not my mother, not even Kelly. So promise
me you won't tell a soul.

CHARLIE
Yeah, of course. What is it?

CLAUDIA
(slowly breaks down)
After the abortion there was some kind of problem. And I had
to go into the hospital and . . . umm . . . there were
complications, and now they say there's a chance I might never
be able to have children.

CHARLIE
Oh Jesus, Claudia. I'm sorry. I didn't know.

CHARLIE gets up and slides into the booth next to CLAUDIA. He puts his
arm around her and pulls her close.

CLAUDIA
It's weird, you know, I never thought I'd want kids until they
told me I might not be able to have them.

CHARLIE
If you think about it, that's true of just about everything.

Neither one of them knows what to say.

CHARLIE
Hey, you think I could get that dance now?

CHARLIE slides out of the booth and pulls her with him. They slowly dance in
the empty bar.

◘EXT: MOTEL. NIGHT

A seedy little beachfront motel. Charlie's car is parked in the lot.

◘INT: MOTEL. NIGHT

CLAUDIA walks out of the bathroom in a slip and slowly walks over to
CHARLIE. They stand in front of each other, both uncomfortable, and then
hesitantly kiss.

◘INT: CLAUDIA AND MICHAEL'S KITCHEN. NIGHT

MICHAEL sits at the kitchen table. He looks at his watch. He gets up, grabs his coat, and storms out, slamming the door behind him.

◘EXT: SUBURBAN STREET. NIGHT

An empty road. MICHAEL'S car flies by.

◘EXT: THE SAND CRAB SALOON. NIGHT

MICHAEL speeds up to the bar and hops out.

◘INT: THE SAND CRAB SALOON. NIGHT

MICHAEL enters the near empty bar and finds GOLDIE watching football.

> MICHAEL
> Hey, Goldie, ya seen Claudia tonight?

> GOLDIE
> Hey Mike, what's going on?

> MICHAEL
> You seen Claudia tonight?

> GOLDIE
> No. Why? What's up?

> MICHAEL
> Do you know if she's with Melissa?

> GOLDIE
> I don't think so. Is everything all right?

> MICHAEL
> No, it's not all right, all right? Fucking motherfucker. I bet she's with that scumbag.

GOLDIE

What the hell are you talking about, man? She's probably with her sister or Teresa.

MICHAEL shakes his head, fuming.

GOLDIE

Maybe you just missed her. Why don't you try home again?

MICHAEL

This is bullshit, man.

◘ INT: THE SAND CRAB SALOON'S PHONE BOOTH. NIGHT

MICHAEL tries their number.

◘ INT: CLAUDIA AND MICHAEL'S HOUSE. NIGHT

The phone just rings and rings until the machine picks up.

◘ INT: THE SAND CRAB SALOON. NIGHT

MICHAEL

She's not there. Where the fuck could she be? It's one o'clock in the morning.

MICHAEL grabs a shot off the bar and downs it.

MICHAEL

Do you know something?

GOLDIE

What would I know?

MICHAEL

Is she with him? Is that what's going on? Is she out fucking around with him tonight?

GOLDIE
Hey, Michael, don't talk about Claudia that way, okay.

MICHAEL
Hey, I don't need to be preached to by you. Okay?
(pause)
This is fucked up, man. This is not right. Is everybody in this
town fucking me behind my back tonight?

GOLDIE shakes his head and won't look at him.

*MICHAEL grabs a beer and throws it against the back wall and storms
out.*

◘INT: MOTEL ROOM. NIGHT

CLAUDIA sits back against the headboard, smoking a cigarette. CHARLIE sits with his legs off the side of the bed, getting dressed. He looks over at her and she says nothing. She then gets up and goes into the bathroom.

◘INT: MOTEL ROOM BATHROOM. NIGHT

CLAUDIA enters the bathroom and closes the door. She then leans back against the door, disappointed in herself.

> CHARLIE
> *(OS)*
> You all right in there?

> CLAUDIA
> Yeah, I'll be right out.

She looks at herself long and hard in the mirror and exits.

◘INT: MICHAEL'S CAR. NIGHT

MICHAEL speeds down the street, close to tears.

◘EXT: TERESA'S FRONT DOOR. NIGHT

MICHAEL knocks on the door. TERESA appears, barely dressed, ready for bed.

> TERESA
> Hey Michael, what's going on?

> MICHAEL
> Hi, Terry, I know it's late, is Claudia here?

> TERESA
> No. Is something wrong? Are you drunk?

MICHAEL

No. I don't know. I can't find her.

TERESA

Did you try Kelly?

MICHAEL

Yeah. I called over there, there's no answer. I went to the bar. She's not there either.

TERESA

Well, she's not there and she's not here. . . . Do you think maybe . . . Do you want to come in?

MICHAEL
(thinks for a bit)
No. Thanks. If you hear from her tell her I'm at home.

TERESA

Hey, Michael, I'm sorry.

MICHAEL

Yeah, me too.

MICHAEL turns and walks down her stoop.

◼ EXT: MOTEL PARKING LOT. NIGHT

CLAUDIA walks from the motel room to Charlie's car and gets in. CHARLIE follows. They pull out.

◼ INT: CHARLIE'S CAR. NIGHT

All sound drops out. CLAUDIA stares out the car window as they drive. CHARLIE reaches out and touches her hand. She looks at it and then at him. She tries to smile and then looks back out the window.

◘EXT: CLAUDIA AND MICHAEL'S STREET. DAWN

CHARLIE'S car pulls down the street and he turns off his lights. He then pulls over and kills the engine.

CLAUDIA opens the door, steps out, and pops her head in the window. She then runs off down the street. Charlie's car pulls away.

◘EXT: CLAUDIA AND MICHAEL'S HOUSE. DAWN

CLAUDIA comes walking back up the alley to her back door. She stops at the door. She then opens it, defeated.

◘INT: CLAUDIA AND MICHAEL'S KITCHEN. DAWN

The house is dark. CLAUDIA enters and MICHAEL is sitting at the kitchen table.

> MICHAEL
> Why are you doing this to me?

> CLAUDIA
> What?

> MICHAEL
> You want to tell me where you were all night?

> CLAUDIA
> I was at work and then I went out with my sister.

> MICHAEL
> You didn't think to maybe call?

> CLAUDIA
> Why would I call?

> MICHAEL
> Oh, I don't know. Maybe I might be worried about you. Maybe I'd like to know where you were?

CLAUDIA

I'm sorry. I just lost track of the time, that's all. Please don't give me a hard time about it.

MICHAEL

Don't give you a hard time? You're gone all day and then you come home at five in the morning and I'm not supposed to give you a hard time? I'm sitting home here alone and I don't know if you're okay or what and I'm not supposed to give you a hard time?
(getting angry)
Do me a favor and sit down here.

CLAUDIA sits opposite MICHAEL.

MICHAEL

Why don't you just tell me where you were all night.

CLAUDIA

I told you I was at work and then I went out.

MICHAEL

I called work and they said you left early. Why'd you leave early?

CLAUDIA

Because it was quiet and I made plans to have dinner with my sister.

MICHAEL

I called your mother's house too, there was no answer.

CLAUDIA

What are you doing calling my mother's house? Are you keeping tabs on me?

MICHAEL
(suddenly yelling)
No, I'm not keeping tabs on you, but like I said before, I didn't hear from you all day. So I got a little fucking concerned.

CLAUDIA

We went out to a bar after dinner and I just lost track of the
time.

MICHAEL

You don't give a fuck about me, do you?

CLAUDIA

Michael, come on.

MICHAEL

I can't take this, Claudia. Why not just be honest with me?

CLAUDIA *doesn't answer. She is starting to get upset.*

MICHAEL

Just answer me. Do you care about me at all, about us?

CLAUDIA

Please, Michael.

MICHAEL

What? I can't hear you? Where were you?

CLAUDIA
(near tears)

I don't know.

MICHAEL

You don't know where you were? Or you don't know about us?
Listen, I'm not gonna let you make a jerkoff outta me. There's
plenty of women out there who would treat me with some
respect; that's all I'm asking for. That's not too fucking much to
ask, is it?
(calms down)
You were with Charlie, right?

CLAUDIA

Michael, let me explain. . . .

MICHAEL

I can't fucking believe this.

MICHAEL slams his fist down on the table. CLAUDIA doesn't move.

> MICHAEL
> *(looking down)*
> Look, just get out of this house. Just get out right now. I don't want to look at your fucking face.

CLAUDIA nods, turns around, and exits.

◘EXT: CLAUDIA AND MICHAEL'S HOUSE. DAWN

CLAUDIA gets in her car and takes off.

◘EXT: BRIDGE. DAWN

CLAUDIA drives over the bridge and out of town. Her car then slows down and pulls over. She thinks for a bit and then makes a U-turn and heads back into town.

◘INT: CLAUDIA'S MOM'S HOUSE. EARLY MORNING

KELLY climbs down the stairs in her robe.

◘INT: CLAUDIA'S MOM'S HOUSE. NIGHT

CLAUDIA sits at the kitchen table. KELLY enters and stands opposite her.

> KELLY
> You want to tell me what's going on?

> CLAUDIA
> I did something pretty awful to Michael tonight.

> KELLY
> How awful?

> CLAUDIA
> You know Charlie moved back home a few weeks ago and . . . I've been sort of seeing him again.

KELLY

Oh, Claudia. One asshole walks out of our life and now you're gonna let another one walk right back in.

CLAUDIA

I don't know if I ever really got over him, Kelly.

KELLY gives her a knowing look.

CLAUDIA

Look, I don't want you to think I feel good about this but I just know that I'm not happy with Michael anymore, you know. I just want a different life than the one I'm living.

KELLY

And you think Charlie's the answer.

CLAUDIA

I was hoping so, but I don't know.

KELLY

Look, I'm not gonna tell you how to live your life but I'll give you the only bit of good advice that Pop ever gave me. He said, "No matter how hard you try, you can't shine shit," and that kid is shit.

◻EXT: DINER. NIGHT

The diner is quiet.

◻INT: DINER. NIGHT

CLAUDIA mops up the floor. She then slumps down into an empty booth and starts to cry.

◻INT: CLAUDIA'S MOM'S KITCHEN. DAY

The phone rings and CLAUDIA enters and answers it in the kitchen. MOM listens.

CLAUDIA

Hello.

▪EXT: BOARDWALK. DAY

CHARLIE is on the phone on the boardwalk.

Crosscut:

CHARLIE

It's me.

CLAUDIA

It's not a good time right now.

CHARLIE

Yeah, well, I'm just calling to see how you're doing. See how your mom is.

▪INT: CLAUDIA'S MOM'S KITCHEN. DAY (CON'T)

CLAUDIA

She's doing much better, thanks.

(beat)

Look, I really gotta go, Charlie. I'm sorry.

CHARLIE

When can I see you again?

CLAUDIA

I don't really know. I need some time. Okay? I got to go.

CHARLIE

Yeah sure. Everything's still cool with us, though, right?

CLAUDIA

Yeah.

CHARLIE

All right.

CLAUDIA hangs up and sits down and exits the kitchen.

◼EXT: FRONT PORCH. SAME DAY

CLAUDIA stands out on the porch. MOM then appears behind her with her walker.

> MOM
> Claudia? Everything all right?

> CLAUDIA
> Yeah, Mom, everything's fine.

> MOM
> Was that your father?

> CLAUDIA
> No.

> MOM
> *(joking)*
> Good. Because you know the next time he calls he's gonna want the house back and we'll be out on the street.

MOM smiles and sits down with CLAUDIA.

> MOM
> Never an easy day, huh?

> CLAUDIA
> *(laughing)*
> Seriously.

> MOM
> *(breathes in)*
> God, that smells good. I've been holed up in this house so long I forgot what the ocean smells like.

CLAUDIA

I guess you're feeling better then, huh Mom?

MOM

Yeah, but what's going on with you?

CLAUDIA

I don't think things are gonna work out with Michael. I can't marry him.

MOM

Yeah, I sort of suspected that.
(beat)
You know, ever since you were a little girl, you were always much more like your father than you were like me. And don't take that the wrong way. I fell in love with him because he was different than anybody else around here. He was a crazy kid with crazy dreams. And I guess I knew what I was getting into when I married him, but you always think you're gonna be the one to change them. But you can't.

MOM looks off and seems lost in her thoughts, then snaps back.

MOM

Anyway, I don't know, what I guess I'm trying to say is I think you're doing the right thing.

◘EXT: CLAUDIA AND MICHAEL'S HOUSE. DAY

CLAUDIA pulls up in her car and gets out. She walks to the back door.

◘EXT: CLAUDIA AND MICHAEL'S DRIVEWAY. DAY

As CLAUDIA approaches the side stoop, MICHAEL comes out of the house on his way to a softball game and stands beside her.

MICHAEL

What are you doing here?

CLAUDIA

Is this a bad time?

MICHAEL

No, it's all right. What's up?

CLAUDIA

I was just thinking we should probably talk soon.

MICHAEL

Yeah, I guess we should. What happened, Claudia? What happened to us?

CLAUDIA

Nothing happened. It just . . . sometimes it just fades away . . . you know.

MICHAEL

So, you just don't love me anymore?

CLAUDIA

Of course I love you. But not in the way you want. It's just . . . I
think the best thing for me right now is to go out and figure out
what I'm going to do with the rest of my life. Figure out who I
am.

MICHAEL

Does Charlie figure into those plans?

CLAUDIA

I'm sorry about that Michael. . . . It was . . .

MICHAEL

No, forget it. I'm sorry. Look, I really don't even want to know.

MICHAEL nods his head telling her he doesn't need to know.

CLAUDIA

Do you understand why I have to do this?

MICHAEL

I guess. I just wish you could be happy here with me but if it
ain't right for you, it ain't right.

CLAUDIA smiles.

MICHAEL

You know, if you ever want to come back, I'll be here.

CLAUDIA
(laughs)

No you won't.
(beat)

Can I get a hug before I go?

MICHAEL gives her a hug and they hold each other for a long time.

▫EXT: BUGSY'S GAS STATION. MORNING

CLAUDIA'S car pulls up to the gas station. She gets out and enters the office.

◼INT: BUGSY'S GAS STATION'S OFFICE. MORNING

CLAUDIA enters and CHARLIE sits at the desk reading a newspaper and drinking coffee.

CHARLIE
(a little pissed off)

Hey, look who it is. Long time, no see.

CLAUDIA

Hi.

CHARLIE

How you been?

CLAUDIA nods.

JOHN CLIFFORD

CHARLIE

Your mom okay?

CLAUDIA

She's coming around.

CHARLIE

That's good.

They are both very uncomfortable.

CHARLIE

So look, I been doing some planning about the trip and I figure
if we're gonna do this we may as well leave next week or so. You
know?

CLAUDIA

Look, Charlie. I don't think that's gonna work out after all.

CHARLIE

What are you talking about?

CLAUDIA

I've been, I just think . . . I don't think it's gonna work.

CHARLIE
(laughing it off)
You don't think it's gonna work? So what the fuck? You gonna
marry Michael after all?

CLAUDIA

No. It doesn't have anything to do with Michael.

CHARLIE

So then . . . what . . . what'd I do wrong?

CLAUDIA

You didn't do anything wrong. I just got some things I got to
figure out. And I got to figure it out on my own. If anybody
could understand that, you could, right?

CHARLIE

I guess this is sorta payback in a way?

CLAUDIA

No, it's nothing like that. This is just me doing what's right for me.

CHARLIE

All right. So I guess I'll see you around.

CLAUDIA

Yeah, I'll see you around.

CHARLIE nods. CLAUDIA turns and heads to the door and opens it. She turns back around to him.

CHARLIE

Hey Claudia. The other night, it wasn't there, was it?

CLAUDIA shakes her head and exits. CHARLIE watches as her car pulls away. He then stands up and pulls the MECHANIC WANTED *sign out of the front window.*

◻EXT: CLAUDIA'S MOM'S HOUSE. DAY

CLAUDIA pulls up and enters the house.

◻INT: CLAUDIA'S MOM'S HOUSE. DAY

CLAUDIA enters and throws her coat on the couch.

She then walks over and sits down at the family's piano. She opens the piano and plays just a few notes. It's clear she can play. She then stops and closes the piano. The camera pans off her to photographs of herself as a young girl and pictures of her mother and father, young, happy, and beautiful.

■EXT: THE TOWN. DAWN

A montage similar to the one that opened the film. However, this time all is quiet.

■INT: CLAUDIA AND MICHAEL'S KITCHEN. DAWN

MICHAEL, dressed for work, sits alone having breakfast.

■INT: KELLY'S BEDROOM. DAWN

KELLY is asleep in bed. MARTY is sitting up in bed putting his boots on. Her baby sleeps next to them in a crib.

■INT: MOM'S BEDROOM. DAWN

MOM sleeps in bed. The TV is on.

■INT: ALICE'S BATHROOM. DAWN

CHARLIE stands at the mirror brushing his teeth with his finger. He throws some water in his hair and quietly steps out of the bathroom.

■INT: ALICE'S BEDROOM. DAWN

CHARLIE softly steps down the hall into her bedroom, grabs his jacket, and heads for the door. ALICE, in bed, looks up.

> ALICE
> You leaving?

> CHARLIE
> Yeah. I got to get to work.

> ALICE

All right.

> CHARLIE

Yeah. I'll see you around.

CHARLIE walks out.

◘EXT: ALICE'S HOUSE. DAWN

CHARLIE steps out into the cold. CHARLIE picks up Alice's newspaper and then walks off her stoop, across the street, up his driveway, and into his mom's house.

◘EXT: BEACH. DAWN

CLAUDIA steps off the boardwalk and onto the beach. She then walks the width of the beach to the shore and stands there.

JOHN CLIFFORD

◘INT: CLAUDIA'S MOM'S HOUSE, BEDROOM. MORNING

CLAUDIA throws some clothes into a suitcase and shuts it. She heads out of her bedroom and down the hallway.

◘INT: CLAUDIA'S MOM'S LIVING ROOM. MORNING

CLAUDIA heads down the stairs and to the door. KELLY appears behind her.

> KELLY
> You going someplace?

CLAUDIA turns.

CLAUDIA

I think so. What do you think?

KELLY

I think you're doing the right thing. I just can't believe it's taken you this long to do it.

CLAUDIA

I'm scared, you know.

KELLY

Who isn't? Is there anything you want me to tell everybody?

CLAUDIA

It doesn't really matter, does it?

KELLY

No, it doesn't.

CLAUDIA

You'll be okay taking care of Mom?

KELLY

Don't worry about Mom, she'll be fine. Now get outta here before you change your mind.

A quick kiss and CLAUDIA exits.

◘EXT: CLAUDIA'S MOM'S HOUSE. MORNING

CLAUDIA throws her suitcase in the trunk, gets in her car, and pulls away.

◾EXT: BUGSY'S GAS STATION. MORNING

CLAUDIA pulls up and slows down in front of the gas station. It's closed. CLAUDIA sighs and pulls off.

◾EXT: BRIDGE. MORNING

CLAUDIA'S car pulls up and over the bridge.

Fade out.

JOHN CLIFFORD